FIRE
AND
SPICE

JOHN GREGORY SMITH

FIRE
AND
SPICE

**FRAGRANT RECIPES FROM
THE SILK ROAD AND BEYOND**

NOURISH
EAT WELL, LIVE WELL

FIRE AND SPICE

JOHN GREGORY-SMITH

First published in the UK and USA in 2019 by
Nourish, an imprint of Watkins Media Limited
Unit 11, Shepperton House, 83–93 Shepperton Road
London N1 3DF

enquiries@nourishbooks.com

Recipes in this book have been previously published in the
following volumes:
Mighty Spice Cookbook by John Gregory-Smith
Mighty Spice Express by John Gregory-Smith

Commissioning Editor: Kate Fox
Managing Editor: Daniel Hurst
Design: Karen Smith
Production: Uzma Taj
Commissioned photography: William Lingwood and Toby Scott

A CIP record for this book is available from the British Library

ISBN: 978-1-84899-376-1

10 9 8 7 6 5 4 3 2 1

Typeset in Harman & Brandon Grotesque
Colour reproduction by XY Digital
Printed in China

Publisher's note

While every care has been taken in compiling the recipes for
this book, Watkins Media Limited, or any other persons who
have been involved in working on this publication, cannot accept
responsibility for any errors or omissions, inadvertent or not,
that may be found in the recipes or text, nor for any problems
that may arise as a result of preparing one of these recipes. If
you are pregnant or breastfeeding or have any special dietary
requirements or medical conditions, it is advisable to consult a
medical professional before following any of the recipes contained
in this book.

Notes on the recipes

The food symbols are used even when only a small amount of an
item is present. Peanuts have been classed as nuts and pine nuts,
quinoa and amaranth as seeds. Dairy free milk, yogurt, cheese and
cream have been classed as either nut- or soya-based. And dairy
free margarine has been classed as nut-, seed- or soya-based.
New products continually come onto the market, however,
making it impossible to be definitive about symbols. So it's vital to
check the manufacturer's labelling carefully before using any food
or drink, since the ingredients used by different brands do change
and vary, especially regarding small quantities of ingredients.
Do be aware, also, that manufacturers are not required to detail
minuscule quantities of ingredients.

Do not mix metric, imperial and US cup measurements:
1 tsp = 5ml 1 tbsp = 15ml 1 cup = 240ml

nourishbooks.com

CONTENTS

INTRODUCTION

Let's start by winding things back ten years to when I first began working on what forms part of this book. To be honest, it wasn't really a book back then but more of a ruse to get me get out of London and go travelling around the world. You see, I needed to escape. Just previous to this, the successful sauce brand that I had spent the past years building up from nothing to the point that it was stocked in supermarkets across the UK had folded. The recession had hit and demand for premium ethnic sauces had nose-dived. I needed a new start, so I did what anyone irresponsible twenty-something would do and fled the country to avoid reality and figure out what on earth I was going to do with myself ...

Now, this is not a sob story, far from it. In actuality, this hiccup, which at the time felt monumental, kickstarted my career as a writer – something that I now know is my true calling and cherish more than anything. To date, I have written five cookbooks, become a specialist in Middle-eastern cuisine and been fortunate enough to write for publications all over the world. Beyond writing, I regularly appear on TV, cooking up a storm or talking about the subject I adore. I also get to go host lively events in fabulous restaurants when I am promoting a new book. I love the buzz of being in the kitchen and nailing a successful dinner service. The rise of social media has also allowed me to reach an even wider audience and my Instagram account and website are fantastic tools for me to showcase recipes and test out new ideas. Have a look: @johngs. In short, what then seemed like a disaster led me to my dream job. I just didn't know it at the time.

If you've ever been travelling solo, you'll know that it's both incredibly rewarding and, at the same time, a bit lonely. You have to make a real effort to find company. Thankfully, when most people see that you are alone they are very willing to extend the hand of friendship and welcome you to their circle. I enjoyed the company but dreaded the opening gambit of getting-to-know-you questions that would inevitably follow. I hadn't yet come to terms with the real reason that I was abroad myself, so I certainly wasn't ready to share it with strangers. To circumnavigate these awkward enquiries, I made up a fake project to justify my travels; I told people I was researching a cookbook about spices and street food that was a cinch to use, and only ever had up to five spices per recipe. It wasn't so far from the truth – after all, spices had been my work and my passion for years, so writing about them didn't seem like too much of a leap! The odd thing was that the more I talked about *The Mighty Spice Cookbook* (yes, I named it very early on – who would believe me without a title?) the more I became invested in it. I'd conjured this book out of thin air, but it was a book that I knew that I would really like to read so, in the end, I decided to knuckle down and write the thing. My little white lie quickly became a reality.

So began a wonderful new chapter of my life. I spent six months travelling around the Far East, South-east Asia, India, The Middle East and Mexico. I learnt about exotic cuisines with local people in far-flung destinations, often working in home kitchens to get to the true heart of the cuisine. I spent time in some of the greatest cities on the planet, eating street food and marvelling at the myriad of sights, sounds and flavours of the world we live in. It's bloody cool! I have always enjoyed travelling but this changed everything. It turns out that this project, conjured out of thin air to justify my travels to a group of strangers, was just what I needed – it gave me a new lease of life and brought the fire back to my belly. Sadly, I didn't quite understand the business of books and when I handed in my neatly organised travel receipts as expenses to my poor publisher, they looked deeply alarmed. This was what my advance was for. Whoops! I got that a bit wrong, but it didn't matter, the project had saved me and I was blissfully happy. It's funny how things pan out, isn't it?

My first book, *The Mighty Spice Cookbook*, was published a few years later in 2011. What a ride; me an unknown with an actual cookbook that real people could buy and not only that, one that they could use to recreate my recipes. *The Mighty Spice Cookbook* flew off the shelves and was sold around the world and I was quickly commissioned to write another. In 2013, *Mighty Spice Express* was born, the premise being the same delicious spice-laden food inspired by my travels, but made speedy.

There are so many key moments from my research travels for these books that it's hard to think where to start. Finding the best restaurants or most notorious home kitchens was harder in those days – you have to understand that this was just at the start of social media being a thing. I had a random account on twitter (a newish platform that utterly mystified me) and though Facebook existed it was mainly used for finding ex colleagues and long-lost school mates to stalk. I found a few blogs to guide me but mainly it was instinctive, meeting people and charming my way into their kitchens.

One of the highlights of those travels was exploring Chengdu in China, a huge city that was being heavily built up to become even more impressive. I was taken in by a warm and welcoming local family where I perfected my twice-cooked pork recipe and learnt the secrets of the tongue tingling Sichuan peppercorn in their cosy apartment in the south of the city (all while somehow remaining oblivious to the fact that I was in the home of the panda!). It was my first experience of authentic home cooked Sichuan food, bold and brash and unlike the Cantonese food I was familiar with. I was enchanted. The balance of flavour and the way they used spices in such clever ways was inspiring.

I had the great fortune of visiting one of the greatest kitchens of them all – the *langar*, set in the Golden Temple in Amritsar, India. This Sikh temple is more beautiful than you can ever imagine, a serene golden shrine floats on a lake in a gleaming white marble sanctuary. The kitchen provides free meals, feeding thousands of worshippers who flock to this sacred place every day. It runs on volunteers, so for two joyous days, I chopped ingredients and stirred vast vats of vegetables curries, cooked in colossal vessels with a mighty spoon the size of an oar. It was a pinch-me moment and one that I will never forget.

I was also lucky enough to go to Sri-Lanka and fell instantly in love with the pearl of the Indian Ocean. It's sun-kissed cities were vibrant and bustling, the people so warm and welcoming. I went to Kandy, a town in the lush mountains, flanked by rainforests and verdant tea plantations, and went on to explore Sigiriya, an ancient fortress built on the top of a massive rock that towers nearly 200 meters (656 feet) above the abundant foliage. I learnt about the Chinese influence on the cuisine and how to make cool coastal curries while I worked my way along the glistening beaches of the south. The island was still recovering from the tsunami that ravaged it in 2004, but it was recovering, and I just know this wonderful place will bounce back again after the recent atrocities.

It was whilst researching these early books that I had my first real flavour of Middle-eastern cuisine, a definite prelude to the direction my career has gone in today. I marvelled at the Medina of Fez, avoiding the donkey-drawn carts that meander through the maze-like alleyways of the city. I have been back time and time again and wondrously the town hasn't changed much in the ten years that I have known it. The street food along the main thoroughfare from the Blue Gate is still the best in the country and you can feast on everything from beautifully spiced kofta sandwiches, thick bissara soup, earthy snails, crispy fried sardines and sticky sweet pastries. It's like going back in time. Extraordinary.

I discovered the ultimate kebab culture in Istanbul, the magnificent city that straddles the mighty Bosporus and is the gateway between the East and the West. Turkish food was such a revelation, a mixture of Mediterranean cuisine, Arabic and opulent Ottoman dishes and in Istanbul all was on offer to sample; stubbly spiced stews from the east of the country, sensational seafood dishes and incredible street food. My favourite has to the lahmacun, a spiced lamb flatbread that is woken up with a squeeze of lemon. Heaven. In Lebanon, I worked as a chef in Beirut for a few weeks so that I could get to know more about the country's regional dishes. It was one of the most rewarding experiences I have ever had. In fact, so enamoured was I with these three countries, I have gone on to write bestselling cookbooks on each destination; *Turkish Delights*, *Orange Blossom and Honey: Magical Moroccan Recipes from the Souks to the Sahara* and *Saffron in the Souks: Vibrant Recipes from the Heart of Lebanon*.

This brings me up to date, a full decade after I seeded a wild idea that grew into the best decision of my life. It was a pleasure to be asked to put this book together, *Fire and Spice*, a greatest-hits from my first two cookbooks, both highlights from one of the most exciting times of my life. The recipes have been tweaked to make them uniform and organised in such a way that allows both books to work harmoniously together. It's been so overwhelming to relive the work that I did all those years ago and wonderful that it is still relevant today.

John Gregory Smith

ABOUT THE AUTHOR

John Gregory-Smith is a best-selling author, presenter and food and travel writer who specialises in Middle Eastern and North African cuisine. He has published five books, including *Saffron in the Souks, Orange Blossom & Honey, Turkish Delights, Mighty Spice Express* and *The Mighty Spice Cookbook*. John appears regularly on Channel 4's *Sunday Brunch* and has recently written for *Condé Nast Traveller, Delicious Magazine, British Airways HighLife, Grazia, Olive Magazine, Out There, Evening Standard* and *Sainsbury's Magazine*.

:camera: @johngs   :bird: @mightyspice   www.johngregorysmith.com

SPICE DIRECTORY

WASABI

The grated root of wasabi, the Japanese member of the horseradish family, is light green in colour and has a strong, peppery flavour. Wasabi comes powdered or in a paste. I prefer to use the paste, as it's quicker to use and lasts well in the fridge. When you think of wasabi you probably think of sushi; however, it's also wonderful in dressings with soy sauce or lime juice, and is delicious mixed into mayonnaise

GARLIC

With its sharp, peppery, pungent taste, garlic is one of the most versatile spices and is an essential ingredient in most spice dishes. Fresh is definitely best, especially when used raw.

GINGER

Delicious in savoury and sweet dishes, this bulbous root has a brilliant fresh, slightly peppery, fragrant taste and a sweet juicy smell.

TURMERIC

A root spice and part of the ginger family, turmeric adds an intense, deep orangey yellow to all dishes it is used in and a distinct earthy and slightly bitter flavour.

TAMARIND

Commonly thought of as a South-east Asian souring agent, tamarind is actually used all over the world from India to Africa and Mexico to the Middle East. It comes from the fruit of a large brown, pea-like pod that is soaked in water. The pulp is squeezed and sieved, and it is the sour water that is used. You can buy good-quality tamarind pastes that you soak in warm water and sieve before using. I'd avoid using tamarind concentrates, which are strong and quite bitter. .

LEMONGRASS

Available fresh, dried and powdered, the delicious, fragrant, lemony flavour of lemongrass comes from the pale-coloured stalk. For maximum clear, lemony aroma and flavour the fresh version is best.

CINNAMON

This fragrant spice has a sweet taste that works superbly in both savoury and sweet dishes. It is available in quills (sticks) or ground.

NUTMEG

Nutmeg is the seed of a small green fruit, which when broken open, reveals a shiny brown, conker-like shell, surrounded by a bright red mesh. The red mesh, once dried, is the spice mace and inside the shell is the nutmeg. Nutmeg is best bought whole and grated as and when required. Nutmeg has a strong fragrance and slightly sweet, spice-heavy flavour that can be used in so many different ways – it flavours biryanis and pilafs everywhere, and works extremely well with traditional white and cheese sauces. It's also delicious in desserts.

ALLSPICE

Allspice was originally named because its flavour was thought to be similar to the combination of several spices including cinnamon, cloves and nutmeg. Allspice is actually a small, dried, unripened fruit, native to central America, and looks a bit like a large, reddish-brown peppercorn. It has a fantastic, aromatic, mixed spice, flavour that is a key ingredient in Caribbean and Middle Eastern cooking. Readily available whole or ground, the whole spice will last about one year in a dry, airtight container, which is kept out of direct sunlight; the ground around six months.

STAR ANISE

A beautiful looking and tasting spice, star anise is often used in fusion cooking to add an intense aniseed flavour and fresh note.

SUMAC

A dried, ground fruit, sumac is used in cooking all over the Middle East. It has a dark red colour and a sour flavour. It is one of the major ingredients in the Arabic Zaatar spice blend used to flavour everything from kebabs to breakfast bread.

SZECHUAN PEPPER

This is the star of Chinese cooking for me, providing a wonderful background heat. Adding a pinch of peppercorns into hot oil will provide you with all the flavour you need for stir-frys and sticky braised meat dishes. They are grainy to eat, so it's better to remove them from the hot oil, once fragrant. You'll still get all the flavour but none of the texture.

BLACK PEPPER

With its spicy pungency, black pepper can add a wonderful kick or gentle warm hint to almost any savoury dish and some sweet dishes, too.

CHILLI

Synonymous with spicy foods, the variety of red and green chillies available provide the choice of adding a warming, mild spicy hint to dishes or a full-on, hot chilli punch.

CURRY LEAVES

These leaves have the flavour of Southern India locked inside them and add a nutty aroma and savoury flavour to a curry. To get the most out of curry leaves, rub them between your hands to break them up as you add them to your curry.

CLOVES

This spice adds a sweet, woody, rich flavour and aroma, but because the flavour is big cloves shouldn't be used too liberally.

SAFFRON

This spice is the bright orange stigma of the purple-coloured saffron crocus. It has a pungent, grassy flavour and adds a rich deep-orange colour to stews, curries and rice dishes. Saffron is very strong and can overpower a dish, so a little goes a long way.

CARDAMOM

The lovely green cardamom pods have a distinctive sweet flavour that is perfect in both sweet and savoury dishes. It is used whole, ground or just for the seeds inside. Cardamom is a key ingredient in many spice blends, but it can be hard to grind into a powder, so remove any little pieces of husk that don't break up after grinding.

VANILLA

This spice, from the orchid family, is a long, thin fruit that when split open, reveals hundreds of tiny black seeds. The seeds can be scraped out and added to a plethora of things to give them an aroma and flavour unlike anything else. You can also buy vanilla extract, and a really good quality one works well; the essence, however, is not worth getting involved with.

FENNEL SEEDS

These are little green-coloured seeds that have an amazing fresh aniseed flavour. Their flavour works incredibly well with pork and fish, and the seeds can be added whole or ground to really lift their flavours.

MUSTARD SEEDS

There are three types of mustard seed: black, brown and white. The brown and white are actually both yellow in colour and are what we know from jars of mustard. You can also buy beautifully golden yellow mustard oil, which is often used in North Indian cuisine. When added to hot oil, they crackle gently and give a nutty, slightly peppery taste that's a great background flavour.

NIGELLA SEEDS

These black seeds are sometimes called black cumin or onion seeds. They have a slightly bitter, oregano herb-like taste and provide a brilliant crunchy texture. Nigella seeds are used extensively in Indian and Middle Eastern cooking, adding flavour to curries, pulses, stews, breads, salads, pickles and chutneys. The seeds are bought whole and can be used without dry roasting, although this will enhance the flavour.

CORIANDER

The mild, slightly orangey, fragrant flavour of coriander comes from the coriander seed and is completely different from the fresh green herb. It can be used whole, crushed or ground in so many ways and is best mates with cumin as far as Indian cooking is concerned. In Thailand it is added to green curry pastes, in Ethiopia the seeds are ground up and added to the Ethiopian spice mix Berbere, and it is an essential part of Arabic Baharat spice blends.

CUMIN

The cumin seed is used whole and ground, and the earthy, nutty flavour and pungent aroma of this spice make it an essential ingredient in most curry powders.

GARAM MASALA

A classic Indian blend of strong spices, garam masala includes cloves, cardamom, cinnamon, nutmeg and black pepper. It's used to give body and depth of flavour to a curry, and is often added at the end of the cooking process to liven things up. There is no standard recipe; it varies from region to region and household to household – everyone has their own version that is always the right one! Thankfully, we can buy good-quality, pre-ground garam masala easily, and it's so worth having. It adds a wonderful hit of spice-heavy seasoning without the need for keeping hundreds of spices on hand. The ground version is also easy to find, but it won't be quite as fragrant as the pre-ground.

PAPRIKA

Made from ground, dry red capsicum peppers, paprika provides a deep-red colour and comes in several different flavours: hot, mild, sweet and smoked. Like all capsicum species, it arrived in Spain from the Americas and its use spread to colour and flavour soups, stews and rice all over the world. The spice works really well in rubs: think Indian tandoori chicken. I really love it mixed with thyme, garlic, lemon juice and olive oil and smothered on any meat, fish or vegetables. Smoked paprika has a much stronger flavour, like a barbecue in a box, and should be used sparingly. The vibrant red colour is a wonderful garnish for salads and dips.

STREET
FOOD

MOROCCAN PAPER BAG SARDINES

SERVES 2
READY IN 15 MINUTES

sunflower oil, for shallow-frying
50g/1¾oz/heaped ⅓ cup plain
  (all-purpose) flour
50g/1¾oz/heaped ⅓ cup
  semolina
2 tsp ground cumin
1 tsp chilli powder
8 small sardines, cleaned
150g/5½oz/scant ⅔ cup yogurt
1 tsp harissa or chilli paste
1 lemon
sea salt

I FIRST ATE THIS FABULOUS SNACK IN FEZ. AFTER A HARD DAY'S EATING, I STOPPED AT A TINY HOLE-IN-THE-WALL WHERE I WAS SERVED CRISPY SARDINES IN A PAPER BAG WITH A WEDGE OF LEMON. WHAT I LOVED WAS THE TEXTURE OF THE BATTER. IT WAS AN EVEN MIX OF FLOUR AND SEMOLINA, WHICH GAVE EVEN MORE CRUNCH TO THE FISH. THE SUBTLE SPICING, WHICH WAS MIXED INTO THE BATTER, REALLY BROUGHT IT TO LIFE. JUST A LITTLE CUMIN AND CHILLI POWDER, AND YOU'RE AWAY.

1 Pour the oil into a large frying pan or skillet to a depth of 1cm/½in and heat over a medium-high heat. Meanwhile, sift the flour into a large mixing bowl and add the semolina, cumin and chilli powder, then season with salt. Pour in 150ml/5fl oz/scant ⅔ cup cold water and whisk into a thick batter. Add the sardines and gently mix to coat them completely in the batter.

2 Shake any excess batter off the sardines and shallow-fry them in the hot oil for 3–4 minutes on each side until beautifully golden and cooked through. Carefully remove the sardines from the oil and put them on to kitchen paper to drain.

3 While the sardines drain, tip the yogurt into a serving bowl and add the harissa. Lightly season with salt and mix well. Cut the lemon into wedges. Serve the sardines with the harissa yogurt and lemon wedges.

CRAB & SPRING ONION PANCAKES

THIS IS A CLASSIC KOREAN SNACK AND ONE THAT I KNOW
YOU'LL LOVE. IT'S ACTUALLY CALLED PA-JUN AND IS AN EGGY
PANCAKE FLAVOURED WITH SOY AND CHILLI, THEN STUFFED
WITH BEAUTIFULLY SWEET CRAB MEAT, FRESH HERBS AND
OYSTER SAUCE. TYPICALLY, IT WOULD BE SERVED WITH
A SPICY KIMCHI – IF YOU CAN GET HOLD OF SOME, GIVE
T A WHIRL. BUT IT REALLY IS JUST SO GOOD ON ITS OWN.

SERVES 2
READY IN 15 MINUTES

40g/1½oz/⅓ cup plain (all-
    purpose) flour
1 egg
¼ tsp crushed chilli flakes
1 tsp light soy sauce
3 spring onions (scallions),
    trimmed and finely chopped
1 handful of coriander (cilantro)
    leaves, finely chopped
100g/3½oz/scant ⅔ cup cooked
    white crab meat
1cm/½in piece fresh root ginger,
    peeled and grated
1 tbsp groundnut (peanut) oil
2 tbsp oyster sauce

1 Tip the flour into a large mixing bowl, pour in
60ml/2fl oz/¼ cup water and crack in the egg. Season
with the chilli flakes and soy sauce, and whisk everything
together into a smooth batter.

2 Put half of the spring onions (scallions) and coriander
(cilantro) in the batter. Mix well. Put the other half into
a separate mixing bowl and add the crab and ginger,
then mix well.

3 Heat half the oil in a large frying pan or skillet over a medium
heat and pour in half the batter mix. Cook for 1 minute on
each side, then transfer to a serving plate. Keep the pancake
warm while you cook a second pancake in the same way.

4 Brush the top of each pancake with a quarter of the oyster
sauce. Divide the crab mixture into 2 portions and arrange
1 portion in a line down the centre of each pancake. Fold the
pancakes in half and transfer them to serving plates. Drizzle
the remaining oyster sauce over each portion and serve.

HUMMUS BEIRUTI

SERVES 2
READY IN 10 MINUTES

4 tbsp olive oil
115g/4oz minced (ground) lamb
¼ tsp ground allspice
¼ tsp ground cumin
a pinch of ground cinnamon
1½ lemons
2 pitta breads
400g/14oz/scant 2 cups tinned
   chickpeas
1 garlic clove
2 tbsp tahini
sea salt

TO ME, HUMMUS ROCKS! MY HUMMUS BEIRUTI IS A SLIGHTLY TARTED-UP VERSION OF THE AWESOME DIP. I MAKE A DELICIOUSLY LIGHT HUMMUS, THEN TOP IT WITH LOVELY SWEET LAMB THAT HAS BEEN FRIED, SUPER-FAST, WITH ALLSPICE, CUMIN AND CINNAMON. THE HIT OF SPICED LAMB MELTS THROUGH THE HUMMUS AND MAKES IT EVEN MORE UNBELIEVABLY TASTY. THIS IS READY IN LESS THAN 10 MINUTES, SO THERE'S ALWAYS TIME FOR A BIT OF HAPPY HUMMUS EATING.

1 Heat 1 tablespoon of the oil in a frying pan or skillet over a high heat and add the lamb. Stir-fry for 2 minutes, then reduce the heat to medium. Add the allspice, cumin and cinnamon, and squeeze in the juice of ½ lemon. Cook for 2–3 minutes, stirring occasionally, until the lamb is cooked through.

2 While the lamb cooks, pop the pitta breads into a toaster and toast until crunchy.

3 Chuck the chickpeas in a colander and give them a good rinse. Drain off any excess water and put them into a blender or food processor with the remaining olive oil. Peel the garlic and add it to the blender with the tahini and 55ml/1¾fl oz/scant ¼ cup water. Season with salt. Squeeze in the juice of the remaining lemon and blend until smooth. Serve the hummus topped with the lamb and with the toasted pitta for dunking.

FRIED CHILLI CORN

A FEW YEARS AGO I WAS IN THAILAND FOR NEW YEAR'S
EVE WITH ALL THE FAMILY. WE STAYED IN A BEAUTIFUL
HOUSE ON PHUKET WHERE WE WERE COMPLETELY SPOILED
BY THE FANTASTIC CHEF, JITTY. JITTY COULD COOK LIKE
AN ANGEL SENT FROM COOKING HEAVEN, AND EVERY MEAL
WAS A COMPLETE PLEASURE TO EAT. SHE REALIZED THAT
SHE HAD A BUNCH OF VERY GREEDY BRITS, WHICH OPENED
UP THE FLOODGATES TO SNACKS THROUGHOUT THE DAY.
HER AWESOME CORN WAS SERVED AS THE SUN WENT DOWN,
WITH AN ICE-COLD BEER BY THE POOL. I CAN'T GIVE YOU THAI
SUNSETS OR A POOL, BUT MAKE THIS CORN, GRAB A BEER
AND YOU'LL BE JUST AS HAPPY.

SERVES 2
READY IN 10 MINUTES

750ml/26fl oz/3 cups
  sunflower oil
250g/9oz/1⅔ cups tinned
  sweetcorn
4 tbsp cornflour (corn starch)
1 tsp chilli powder
1 tsp Chinese five-spice powder
sea salt

1 Heat the oil in a deep pan over a high heat. Meanwhile,
  drain the sweetcorn thoroughly in a colander. Tip it into
  a mixing bowl and add the cornflour (corn starch), chilli
  powder, Chinese five-spice powder and 1½ tablespoons
  cold water. Mix everything together well so that the
  sweetcorn is completely coated with the cornflour
  and spices.

2 Using a slotted spoon, carefully transfer the corn to the
  hot oil. Stir, then deep-fry for 3 minutes, or until golden
  and crunchy. Remove from the oil and drain very well on
  kitchen paper. Tip the sweetcorn into serving bowls and
  season with salt. Serve with ice-cold beers.

CHA CA LA VONG – VIETNAMESE TURMERIC & CHILLI SPICED COD

SERVES 4
READY IN 15 MINUTES

SERVES 4
READY IN 15 MINUTES

50g/1¾oz/⅓ cup unsalted peanuts, chopped
250g/9oz rice noodles
6 tbsp vegetable oil
1 handful dill, chopped
1 handful coriander (cilantro) leaves, chopped
1 handful mint leaves, chopped
1 tbsp turmeric
4 tbsp plain (all-purpose) flour
4 cod fillets, about 200g/7oz each, skinned and cut into bite-sized pieces
8–10 spring onions (scallions), halved and finely sliced lengthways
2 tbsp fish sauce
juice of ½ lime
½ red chilli, deseeded and finely chopped

CHA CA LA VONG IS A FAMOUS RESTAURANT IN HANOI THAT SERVES JUST ONE DISH: 'CHA CA' OR FRIED FISH. IT IS SERVED WITH SPRING ONIONS (SCALLIONS) AT YOUR TABLE IN A FRYING PAN, SIZZLING ON TOP OF A SMALL BARBECUE.

1 Heat a frying pan or skillet over a medium heat. Add the peanuts and gently toast, shaking the pan occasionally, for 2–3 minutes, or until the peanuts are a beautiful golden brown. Transfer the nuts to a plate to cool.

2 Cook the noodles according to the packet instructions, drain and immediately refresh under cold water. Drain well then transfer to a bowl, dress with 2 tablespoons of the oil to stop them sticking and set aside. Put the dill, coriander (cilantro) and mint together into one bowl and the peanuts into another.

3 In a large mixing bowl mix together the turmeric and flour. Dip the cod pieces into the flour, making sure every piece is completely coated.

4 Heat the remaining oil in a large frying pan over a medium heat and fry the cod, turning occassionally, for 2–3 minutes, or until the flesh turns opaque and is flaky to the touch.

5 Add the spring onions (scallions), fish sauce and lime juice and gently mix until well combined.

6 Scatter the red chilli over the top and serve with the noodles, herbs and peanuts on the side to mix together as you like.

VIETNAMESE BUN CHA

1 Pour the stock and 500ml/17fl oz/2 cups water into a saucepan and add the peppercorns, star anise, cinnamon stick, sugar and fish sauce. Bash the fat ends of the lemongrass stalks with a spoon, snap them in half and add them to the stock. Add the lime juice, mix well and bring to the boil over a medium heat.

2 Meanwhile, add the noodles to a pan of boiling water and leave to stand for 3 minutes, or as directed on the packet. Drain in a colander and refresh under cold water, then drain again. Leave them in the colander to drain.

3 To make the pork burgers, put the herbs, pork and fish sauce in a large bowl and mix well. Heat the oil in a frying pan or skillet over a medium heat. Meanwhile, divide the pork into 4 and flatten into mini burger shapes. Fry the burgers for 3 minutes on each side, or until golden and cooked through.

4 While the pork is cooking, trim the spring onions (scallions), then cut each in half and then into thin strips. Deseed the chilli, then slice it finely. Cut the lime into 2 pieces.

5 Divide the noodles and bean sprouts between two large serving bowls, and put 2 pork burgers into each bowl. Scatter half the spring onions and the chilli over each bowl, then top with the lime and the herbs. Remove the spices from the stock and divide the hot, fragrant soup between the two bowls. Serve immediately.

SERVES 2
READY IN 20 MINUTES

500ml/17fl oz/2 cups chicken
   stock
6 black peppercorns
2 star anise
2.5cm/1in cinnamon stick
2 tsp sugar
3 tbsp fish sauce
2 lemongrass stalks
juice of ½ lime
140g/5oz vermicelli rice noodles
4 spring onions (scallions)
½ red chilli
½ lime
140g/5oz/1½ cups bean sprouts
1 large handful of coriander
   (cilantro) leaves
1 large handful of mint leaves

For the pork burgers
1 small handful of coriander
   (cilantro) leaves, finely
   chopped
1 small handful of mint leaves,
   finely chopped
120g/4¼oz minced (ground)
   pork
1 tsp fish sauce
1 tsp groundnut (peanut) oil

OAXACA TOSTADAS

SERVES 2
READY IN 15 MINUTES

2 tbsp olive oil

2 large tortillas

1 red onion, peeled and finely
  sliced

2 garlic cloves, peeled and
  roughly chopped

200g/7oz chorizo, roughly
  chopped

2 ripe avocados

1 green chilli

8 spring onions (scallions),
  trimmed

1 handful of coriander (cilantro)
  leaves

1½ limes

1 tomato

55g/2oz Gruyère cheese

a pinch of smoked paprika

sea salt

MY TOSTADAS WERE INSPIRED BY THE WONDERFUL GIANT
TOSTADAS OF THE CENTRAL MARKET IN THE CITY OF OAXACA
IN MEXICO. THEY ARE COMPLETELY DELICIOUS – YOU TASTE
HOT AND COLD, CRUNCHY AND SMOOTH, SPICY AND MILD,
SALTY AND SOUR IN EVERY BITE. AND, AS THEY ONLY TAKE
15 MINUTES TO MAKE, THEY ARE A REAL MIDWEEK LIFESAVER.

1 Preheat the grill (broiler) to high. Meanwhile, brush 1
tablespoon of the oil over both sides of each tortilla. Put them
on to a grill rack and grill (broil) for 30 seconds–1 minute on
each side until crispy and golden at the edges. Remove from
the grill and put on to serving plates.

2 Heat the remaining oil in a frying pan over a medium heat
and add the red onion, garlic and chorizo. Mix well and cook
for 5–6 minutes, stirring occasionally, until golden.

3 Meanwhile, cut the avocados in half and remove the stones
using a knife. Scoop the flesh out with a spoon and put it
into a mini food processor or blender. Cut the top off the
chilli and add to the the food processor with the sping onions
(scallions), coriander (cilantro) and a pinch of salt. Squeeze
in the juice from ½ lime and blend into a rough paste.

4 Finely slice the tomato, grate the cheese and cut the
remaining lime into quarters. Divide the avocado mixture
between the 2 tortillas and spread evenly over, using a knife.
Top with the tomato slices, hot chorizo and onion, and scatter
over the cheese. Give both tostadas a dusting of smoked
paprika and serve with lime wedges.

TURKISH LUHMACUN

1 Preheat the grill (broiler) to high. Meanwhile, heat 1 tablespoon of the oil in a large frying pan or skillet over a high heat. Add the lamb and stir well. Peel and crush over the garlic, and add the paprika, cumin and cinnamon, then season with salt. Squeeze over the juice of ½ lemon and stir-fry for 3–4 minutes until the lamb is cooked through and golden. Remove from the heat and leave to one side.

2 Squeeze out the seeds from the tomato half, then finely chop the flesh. Chuck the tomato into the cooked lamb and add the sun-dried tomato paste. Mix well.

3 Put the tortillas on to a grill rack and brush with the remaining oil. Spoon over the spicy lamb and grill for 1–2 minutes until the tortillas start to crisp up at the edges.

4 While the lahmacun cooks, finely chop the herbs and cut the remaining lemon half into quarters. Scatter the herbs and chilli flakes over the cooked lahmacun and serve with the lemon wedges.

SERVES 2
READY IN 10 MINUTES

1½ tbsp olive oil
200g/7oz minced lamb
2 garlic cloves
½ tsp sweet paprika
½ tsp ground cumin
¼ tsp ground cinnamon
1 lemon
½ tomato
1 tbsp sun-dried tomato paste
2 flour tortillas
1 small handful of mint leaves
1 small handful of parsley leaves
a pinch of crushed chilli flakes
sea salt

DUCK & BLACK BEAN TOSTADAS

SERVES 4
READY IN 35 MINUTES

4 duck breasts (about 150g/
    5½oz each)
4 garlic cloves, crushed
2 tsp smoked paprika
½ tsp chilli powder
4 tbsp olive oil
400g/14oz/2 cups tinned
    black beans
1½ tsp ground cumin
juice of ½ lime
sea salt and freshly ground
    black pepper
1 lettuce, finely sliced, to serve
2 large handfuls of coriander
    (cilantro) leaves, chopped,
    to serve
4 large tortillas, to serve

For the salsa
1 red onion, peeled and
    quartered
115g/4oz/heaped ¾ cup drained
    sun-dried tomatoes in oil
1 tsp smoked paprika
juice of ½ lime

1 Preheat the oven to 200°C/400°F/Gas 6. Trim and score the skin on the duck breasts, and put them in a small roasting tin. Add the garlic, smoked paprika, chilli powder, two tablespoons of the oil and a good pinch of salt. Mix well so that the duck is completely coated. Turn the duck skin-side up, then roast for 25–30 minutes until golden on the outside and juicy and pink in the centre.

2 Meanwhile, drain and rinse the beans and tip them into a saucepan over a medium heat. Mash the beans, using a potato masher, until fairly smooth, then add 55ml/1¾fl oz/ scant ¼ cup water, the rest of the olive oil and the cumin. Add the lime juice, season with salt and pepper, and mix well. Bring to the boil, reduce the heat to low and cook for 8–10 minutes, stirring occasionally, until warmed through and thick. Remove from the heat, cover and leave to one side.

3 To make the salsa, put the onion sun-dried tomatoes, smoked paprika and a pinch of salt into a food processor. Add the lime juice, blend until smooth, then pour into a serving bowl.

4 Finely slice the lettuce and coriander (cilantro), then put them on to a serving plate. Put the tortillas on four serving plates and cover each one with the beans. Slice up the duck and put on top of the beans. Serve with the salad and salsa.

MANOCHE

SERVES 4
READY IN 10 MINUTES

2 tbsp dried thyme
1½ tsp ground cumin
½ tsp ground allspice
¼ tsp chilli powder
4 tbsp olive oil
4 large flour tortillas
200g/7oz cherry tomatoes,
    halved
200g/7oz mozzarella, thinly
    sliced
1 large handful mint leaves,
    roughly chopped
sea salt
lemon wedges, to serve

IN BEIRUT I WORKED AT A BEAUTIFUL BRASSERIE CALLED
SOUK EL TAYEB. NORMALLY, I DIDN'T EAT BREAKFAST BECAUSE
I ATE SO MUCH AND SO WELL DURING THE DAY. ONE MORNING,
HOWEVER, I WAS SO HUNGRY THAT I ASKED THE GUYS FOR
BREAKFAST, WHICH TURNED OUT TO BE MY NEW 'BREAKFAST
OF CHAMPIONS': A FRESHLY COOKED FLAT BREAD, SMOTHERED
IN SPICES AND FILLED WITH CHEESE AND FRESH MINT. I WAS
INSTRUCTED TO OPEN IT UP AND DOUSE IT WITH CHILLI AND
LEMON JUICE BEFORE TUCKING IN. IT WAS A WONDROUS
CULINARY EXPERIENCE AND HERE IS MY VERSION.

1 Preheat the oven to 220°C/420°F/Gas 7. Mix the thyme,
cumin, allspice, chilli powder, oil and a pinch of salt together
in a bowl. Lay out the tortillas on a grill rack and brush the
tops with the flavoured oil. Divide the cherry tomatoes and
mozzarella into four and arrange over the top of each tortilla.

2 Put the grill rack with the pizzas in the oven and cook for 5–6
minutes, or until the bread has gone really crispy at the edges
and the cheese has melted. Scatter over the fresh mint leaves
and serve immediately with wedges of lemon to squeeze over
the top.

SALADS

LITTLE SOUTH ISLAND PORK SALAD

THIS DISH SUMS UP WHY EATING REAL CHINESE FOOD IS SUCH A PLEASURE. NO NUCLEAR-RED GLOOPY SAUCE, NOT A TINNED PINEAPPLE CHUNK IN SIGHT – JUST SIMPLE, FRESH, CLEAN FLAVOURS THAT ALL WORK SUPERBLY TOGETHER AND TAKE MINUTES TO MAKE. THE CRUNCHY FENNEL AND SWEET CARROT SOAK UP ALL THE RICHNESS OF THE STIR-FRIED PORK AND THE DELICIOUS FLAVOURS OF THE TART DRESSING. THIS IS HOW CHINESE FOOD SHOULD BE!

1 Heat a wok over a high heat until smoking. Pour in the oil, swirl it round and then add the pork. Stir-fry for 5–6 minutes until the edges of the pork start to catch and become golden.

2 Sprinkle in the chinese five-spice powder and chilli flakes, then add the soy sauce. Continue to stir-fry for 30 seconds, then remove from the heat and leave to one side.

3 Using a sharp knife, cut the top and bottom off the orange, and stand it up on your chopping board. Carefully slice the skin off in sections, cutting from top to bottom. Remove any remaining pith, then cut out the juicy pieces of orange from the membrane and put them in a mixing bowl. Squeeze in the juice from the membrane.

4 Finely slice the fennel and add it to the bowl with the orange. Peel the carrot and grate it, using the coarse setting on a grater, into the bowl. Pour in the cider vinegar and soy sauce for the dressing, then peel and grate in the ginger, using the fine setting. Put the lettuce leaves and cooked pork, along with all the lovely juices, into the mixing bowl with the salad. Toss everything together and serve.

SERVES 2
READY IN 20 MINUTES

For the pork salad
1 tbsp groundnut (peanut) oil
350g/12oz minced pork
½ tsp Chinese five-spice powder
½ tsp crushed chilli flakes
1 tbsp light soy sauce
1 orange
1 fennel bulb
1 carrot
100g/3½oz frisée lettuce

For the ginger dressing
1½ tbsp cider vinegar
2 tsp light soy sauce
1cm/½in piece fresh root ginger

INDIAN CHICKEN, POMEGRANATE & HERB SALAD

SERVES 4
READY IN 50 MINUTES

500g/1lb 2oz skinless, boneless chicken breasts, cut into bite-sized pieces
2 tbsp olive oil
1 pomegranate
2 large handfuls mint leaves, roughly chopped
2 large handfuls coriander (cilantro) leaves, roughly chopped
3 large carrots, peeled and grated
juice of 1 lemon

For the spice paste
2 tbsp olive oil
½ tsp turmeric
½ tsp mild chilli powder
1 tsp garam masala
2 garlic cloves
1 tsp sea salt

1 To make the spice paste, put all the ingredients in a mini food processor and grind to a smooth paste. Scrape the paste into a mixing bowl, add the chicken and mix well, making sure the chicken is completely coated. Cover and leave for 30 minutes, or overnight in the refrigerator if time allows.

2 Heat the oil in a frying pan over a medium heat. Add the chicken and cook for 5–6 minutes on each side, or until golden, crispy and cooked through.

3 Roll the pomegranate back and forth a couple of times on a hard surface to loosen the seeds, then cut it in half. Using a wooden spoon, bash the seeds out into a bowl. This can get quite messy, so wear an apron to cover your clothes and put the bowl into the sink while you're bashing – this way any mess can easily be washed away. Remove any white bits from the seeds and sieve out the excess juice.

4 Transfer the pomegranate seeds to a serving bowl along with the mint, coriander (cilantro), carrots and lemon juice and mix well. Scatter the cooked chicken pieces and any juices over the top and serve immediately.

GREAT EASTERN DUCK SALAD

SERVES 2
READY IN 25 MINUTES

1 tbsp olive oil
2 duck breasts (about
    165g/5¾oz each)
350g/12oz watermelon
½ red chilli
½ lime
2 tbsp hoisin sauce
1 tsp light soy sauce
¼ tsp Chinese five-spice powder
75g/2½oz/2½ cups watercress
1 handful of mint leaves
55g/2oz/heaped ⅓ cup cashew
    nuts
sea salt

1 Heat the oil in a frying pan over a high heat. Meanwhile, score the fat on the duck breasts and season both sides with salt. Carefully put the duck in the hot pan, skin-side down, and reduce the heat to medium. Cook for 8–10 minutes until the skin is really crispy.

2 While the duck cooks, peel the watermelon and cut it into bite-sized pieces, removing any obvious pips as you go. Chuck the watermelon into a large mixing bowl and leave to one side.

3 Turn the crispy duck over and cook for another 8–10 minutes until beautifully tender and pink in the centre, then remove from the heat.

4 Deseed and finely slice the chilli while the duck finishes cooking. Put it in the mixing bowl with the melon and squeeze over the juice from the lime.

5 Pour out any excess fat from the cooked duck. Add the hoisin sauce, soy sauce and Chinese five-spice powder to the pan, and mix well. Remove the duck breasts from the pan, slice them into thick pieces and leave to one side. Put the watercress, mint and cashew nuts in the bowl with the watermelon, then toss everything together. Serve the salad with the beautiful duck slices, with the juices from the pan spooned over.

ROASTED RED PEPPER & GRILLED MONKFISH SALAD

SERVES 4
READY IN 40 MINUTES

350g/12oz monkfish fillets,
 skinned and boned
70g/2½oz rocket (arugula)
1 small handful parsley leaves,
 finely chopped

For the dressing
2 red chillies
2 red (bell) peppers, quartered
 and deseeded
2 garlic cloves, unpeeled
1 tbsp olive oil, plus extra for
 brushing
100ml/3½fl oz/⅓ cup natural
 yogurt
¼ tsp smoked paprika
juice of 1 lemon
sea salt and freshly ground black
 pepper

1 Preheat the oven to 200°C/400°F/Gas 6. To make the dressing, prick the red chillies with a sharp knife to stop them exploding in the oven, then put in a roasting tray with the red peppers and garlic. Drizzle over the oil, season with a good pinch of salt and pepper and mix well with your hands. Roast for 20–25 minutes, or until everything is golden and the peppers are beautifully soft and sweet. Set aside to cool.

2 Once cool enough to handle, finely chop half the (bell) peppers and put them in a medium-sized mixing bowl. Roughly chop the other half into bite-sized pieces and set aside. Cut off the tops of the chillies and carefully peel away their skins. Slice open, scrape out and discard the seeds, then put the chilli flesh in a mini food processor. Squeeze the garlic cloves out of their skins and add to the mini food processor. Season with a pinch of salt and pepper and grind to a smooth paste. Transfer to the mixing bowl with the finely chopped peppers, then tip in the yogurt, paprika and lemon juice. Mix well and set aside.

3 Preheat the grill (broiler) to high. Brush the monkfish with a little oil and place under the hot grill for 3–4 minutes on each side, or until the flesh has gone milky white and is firm to the touch. Finely slice the monkfish and carefully toss it in the dressing.

4 To serve, toss the rocket (arugula), parsley and remaining peppers together and divide onto four plates. Spoon the tender, creamy monkfish on top and serve immediately with any remaining dressing dolloped over.

CARROT, APPLE & BLACK PEPPER SALAD WITH SEARED TUNA

SERVES 4
READY IN 25 MINUTES

4 garlic cloves
1 tsp coarsely ground black pepper
1 tsp chilli flakes
4 tbsp olive oil
1 tsp sea salt
¼ tsp sugar
4 tuna steaks, 150g/5½oz each

For the salad
50g/1¾oz/⅓ cup unsalted peanuts
2 tomatoes, deseeded and finely sliced
2 apples, quartered, cored, finely sliced and drizzled in lime juice to stop them discolouring
4 large carrots, peeled and grated
3 spring onions (scallions), finely sliced
2 red chillies, deseeded and finely sliced
1 handful mint leaves, finely chopped
1 large handful coriander (cilantro) leaves, roughly chopped

For the dressing
juice of 2 limes
1 tbsp fish sauce
1 tbsp sugar

1 Heat a frying pan or skillet over a medium heat. Add the peanuts and gently toast, shaking the pan occasionally, for 2–3 minutes, or until the peanuts are a beautiful golden brown. Transfer the nuts to a plate to cool.

2 Put the garlic in a mini food processor and blend to a smooth paste. Tip in the black pepper, chilli flakes, 2 tablespoons of the oil, the salt and sugar and blend to a coarse paste. Rub the paste all over the tuna steaks and leave to marinate for 10 minutes. Rinse the mini food processor.

3 Whisk the dressing ingredients together in a large mixing bowl. Give the toasted peanuts a quick blast in a mini food processor until coarsely ground, then add to the mixing bowl along with the other salad ingredients. Toss together with the dressing so that the wonderfully sour Thai flavours in the dressing coat everything.

4 Heat a large griddle pan over a medium heat and add the remaining 2 tablespoons of oil. Fry the tuna steaks for 1–2 minutes on each side, or until turning golden in colour. Remove the griddle pan from the heat but leave the tuna in the pan for another 1–2 minutes. This will ensure the tuna is beautifully seared on the outside but still pink in the middle.

5 Divide the salad onto four serving bowls. Slice each tuna steak into four pieces and place on top of each salad. Serve immediately.

CRAYFISH, PINK GRAPEFRUIT & GLASS NOODLE SALAD

1 Put the noodles into a heatproof bowl and cover with boiling water. Cover and leave to one side for 2–3 minutes to soften. Once soft, drain in a colander and rinse with cold water. Drain again and squeeze out any excess water with your hands so that they are really dry. Leave to one side.

2 Make the dressing while the noodles soften. Remove the tough outer leaves from the lemongrass and cut off the ends of the stalks. Starting at the fatter end, roughly slice each lemongrass stalk into rings. You should see a purple band in the rings. Stop slicing when there are no more purple bands, then discard the rest of the lemongrass, as it will be too tough to eat.

3 Give the lemongrass slices a quick blast in a mini food processor until they are very finely chopped, then tip them into a large mixing bowl. Squeeze the juice from the limes into the bowl with the lemongrass and add the chilli powder, sugar and oil. Whisk everything together to get the flavours going.

4 Using a sharp knife, cut the top and bottom off the grapefruit, then stand it up on your chopping board. Carefully slice the skin off in sections, cutting from top to bottom. Remove any remaining pith, then cut out the juicy pieces of grapefruit from the membrane and put them into the bowl with the dressing. Squeeze in the juice from the membrane. Trim and finely slice the spring onions (scallions), then add them to the bowl. Chuck in the pea shoots, crayfish, basil, mint and cooked noodles. Toss everything together well. Serve with the pumpkin seeds scattered over the top.

SERVES 2
READY IN 15 MINUTES

For the glass noodle salad
140g/5oz vermicelli rice noodles
1 pink grapefruit
2 spring onions (scallions)
30g/1oz pea shoots
150g/5½oz cooked, peeled
   crayfish tails
1 small handful of basil leaves
1 small handful of mint leaves
2 tbsp pumpkin seeds

For the lemongrass dressing
2 lemongrass stalks
2 limes
¼ tsp chilli powder
2 tsp sugar
1 tbsp olive oil

SQUID & CHORIZO SALAD

SERVES 4
READY IN 20 MINUTES

350g/12oz baby squid, cleaned
2 tbsp olive oil
100g/3½oz chorizo, roughly
    chopped
juice of 1 lime
140g/5oz/heaped 1 cup pitted
    black olives, roughly chopped
1 red onion, finely chopped
2 large handfuls parsley leaves,
    roughly chopped
1 red chilli, deseeded and cut
    into fine strips
sea salt and freshly ground black
    pepper

THIS IS SUCH A VIBRANTLY COLOURED SALAD, PACKED FULL OF DIFFERENT TEXTURES AND FLAVOURS THAT EXCITE THE PALETTE. THE FRESH CHILLI, OLIVES, RED ONION AND PARSLEY CREATE AN EASTERN MEDITERRANEAN BASE, BUT IT'S THE CHORIZO THAT'S THE REAL STAR. IT ADDS CRISPINESS, WHICH WORKS WELL WITH THE SOFT SQUID, AND OFFERS LOADS OF FLAVOUR FROM ALL THE PAPRIKA AND SPICES THAT OOZE WHEN IT'S COOKED. THE FRESH LIME JUICE THEN BRINGS THE WHOLE SALAD TOGETHER.

1 Slice the squid into rings, keeping the tentacles whole.

2 Heat the oil in a large frying pan over a medium heat, then add the chorizo. Cook for 3–4 minutes, or until the chorizo starts to turn golden and crispy, stirring occasionally. Scatter the squid into the same pan and stir thoroughly. Cook for 2–3 minutes, or until the squid is pale and cooked through. Remove the pan from the heat, add the lime juice and set aside until you are ready to eat.

3 To assemble the salad, put the squid, chorizo and their juices into a serving bowl. Add the olives, onion, parsley and red chilli and season with a good pinch of salt and pepper. Toss everything together so that the lovely spicy red chorizo and fresh lime juices coat all the other ingredients and serve immediately.

FETA, WALNUT & NIGELLA SEED SALAD

SERVES 4
READY IN 10 MINUTES

50g/1¾ oz/scant ½ cup walnuts,
  roughly chopped
200g/7oz feta
1 green chilli, deseeded and
  finely chopped
1 large handful tarragon leaves,
  roughly chopped
2 large handfuls parsley leaves,
  roughly chopped
2 large handfuls mint leaves,
  roughly chopped
1 tsp nigella seeds

For the dressing
juice of 1 lemon
2 tbsp olive oil
4 spring onions (scallions),
  finely sliced
sea salt and freshly ground
  black pepper

1 To make the dressing, whisk the oil and lemon juice in a bowl and season with a good pinch of salt and pepper. Add the spring onions (scallions) and set aside for 5 minutes to take the rawness out of the spring onions.

2 Put half the chopped walnuts in a large mixing bowl and crumble in half the feta. Pour over the dressing, chuck in the green chilli, tarragon, parsley and mint, then toss everything together.

3 Divide the salad onto four serving plates, scatter the nigella seeds and the remaining walnuts and feta cheese over the top and serve immediately.

POMEGRANATE, FENNEL, ORANGE *&* WATERCRESS SALAD

THIS IS A GREAT-LOOKING FRESH SALAD, BEJEWELLED WITH POMEGRANATE SEEDS AND ORANGE SEGMENTS. IT SHOWCASES THE LOVELY FRESH ANISEED FLAVOUR THAT COMES FROM THE FINELY SHAVED FENNEL AND LIGHTLY CRUSHED FENNEL SEEDS, WHICH ARE USED IN THE DRESSING AND BRING EVERYTHING TOGETHER.

1 To make the dressing, whisk all the ingredients together in a mixing bowl, season with a good pinch of salt and pepper and set aside.

2 Roll the pomegranate back and forth a couple of times on a hard surface to loosen the seeds, then cut it in half. Using a wooden spoon, bash the seeds out into a bowl. This can get quite messy, so wear an apron to cover your clothes and put the bowl into the sink while you're bashing – this way any mess can easily be washed away. Remove any white bits from the seeds and drain off the excess juice. Transfer the seeds into a mixing bowl along with the orange segments, red chilli, watercress and fennel.

3 Pour the dressing over the salad, toss well and serve immediately.

SERVES 4
READY IN 10 MINUTES

1 pomegranate
3 oranges, peeled and cut into segments
½ red chilli, deseeded and finely chopped
75g/2½oz watercress
1 fennel bulb, very finely sliced or shaved with a mandolin

For the dressing
1 tsp fennel seeds, lightly crushed
juice of 1 lemon
2 tbsp orange juice
1 tbsp olive oil
sea salt and freshly ground black pepper

CHINESE TIGER SALAD

SERVES 4
READY IN 10 MINUTES

6 spring onions (scallions),
    finely sliced on a diagonal
1 red (bell) pepper, deseeded
    and finely sliced
1 green (bell) pepper, deseeded
    and finely sliced
2 baby leeks, halved lengthways
    and finely sliced
2 large handfuls coriander
    (cilantro) leaves, finely
    chopped
1 red chilli, finely sliced
sesame seeds, to serve

For the dressing
2 tbsp soy sauce
1 tbsp rice wine vinegar
1 tsp sesame oil
1 tbsp sesame seeds
½ tsp chilli flakes

THIS CRUNCHY SALAD IS ONE OF MY FAVOURITE SIDE DISHES. IN CHINA IT IS SERVED AS AN APPETIZER TO SNACK ON WITH A DRINK OR TO GO WITH KEBABS. IT'S ALSO THE PERFECT ACCOMPANIMENT TO A PIPING HOT STIR-FRY AND RICE. I ALWAYS MAKE ENOUGH TO ROLL UP IN TORTILLA WRAPS WITH CHICKEN FOR LUNCH THE NEXT DAY.

1 Whisk the dressing ingredients together in a large bowl.

2 Add the spring onions (scallions), red and green (bell) peppers, baby leeks, coriander (cilantro) and red chilli, then mix everything together until well combined. Scatter over additional sesame seeds and serve.

KERABU COCONUT & CHILLI SALAD

1 To make the dressing, whisk the fish sauce, lime juice and sugar together in a large bowl. Grate the ginger into the bowl, discarding the fibrous bits, and mix well.

2 Scatter the onion over the dressing and mix well, then set aside for 5–10 minutes. This will take the rawness out of the onion.

3 Meanwhile, toast the coconut in a small frying pan or skillet over a medium heat, stirring continuously, for 30–40 seconds, or until the coconut turns a lovely golden brown. Tip onto a plate and set aside.

4 To assemble the salad, add the red (bell) pepper, bean sprouts, red chilli and mint to the onion mixture and toss until all the ingredients are well coated. Transfer to a serving bowl, scatter the roasted coconut over the top and serve immediately.

SERVES 4
READY IN 10 MINUTES

½ red onion, finely sliced
2 tbsp desiccated coconut
1 red (bell) pepper, deseeded and finely sliced
200g/7oz/scant 2¼ cups bean sprouts
½ red chilli, deseeded and finely chopped
1 small handful mint leaves, roughly chopped

For the dressing
4 tbsp fish sauce
juice of 2 limes
2 tsp sugar
2.5cm/1in piece root ginger, peeled

JETALAH SALAD

SERVES 4
READY IN 15 MINUTES

½ red onion, finely sliced
6 tbsp rice wine or cider vinegar
2 tsp sugar
½ pineapple, peeled
½ cucumber, halved lengthways
1 large tomato, deseeded and
   roughly chopped
1 red chilli, deseeded and finely
   sliced
1 tbsp freshly ground black
   pepper
sea salt

THIS DELICIOUS MALAY SALAD WILL BRING A LITTLE SUNSHINE TO YOUR TABLE. NAZ, A FANTASTIC CHEF AND FRIEND OF MINE, TAUGHT ME HOW TO MAKE THIS SALAD WHEN WE COOKED A MEAL TOGETHER IN THE MOST BEAUTIFUL SPICE GARDEN IN PENANG. WE ATE OUR DINNER SITTING ON A TERRACE OVERLOOKING THE OCEAN, WITH THE SUN GOING DOWN AND THE AIR THICK WITH THE SMELL OF CARDAMOM, CLOVES AND CINNAMON.

1 Put the onion, vinegar and sugar in a large mixing bowl. Season with a pinch of salt, mix well and set aside for 5–10 minutes. This will take the rawness out of the onion.

2 Cut the pineapple into quarters, remove and discard the hard central core from each piece and cut each piece into thin slices. Next, run a teaspoon down the middle of the 2 halves of cucumber, removing the seeds as you go. Slice into thin half-moon pieces.

3 Put the pineapple, cucumber, tomato, red chilli and black pepper into the bowl with the onion mixture, toss everything together until well combined and serve immediately.

FATTOUSH SALAD

THIS IS ONE OF THOSE PERFECT DISHES. IT IS FULL OF SWEET
AND JUICY VEGETABLES THAT ARE COMPLEMENTED WITH
A BEAUTIFULLY TANGY DRESSING THAT IS MADE WITH BOTH
LEMON AND SUMAC. IT LOOKS FANTASTIC AND, WITH ALL THE
DIFFERENT TEXTURES, IT IS INTERESTING TO EAT, TOO. IT IS
EXTREMELY REFRESHING ON A HOT DAY AND ON COLD DAYS
IT BRINGS THE SUNSHINE STRAIGHT TO YOU. WHILE DELICIOUS
EATEN ON ITS OWN, IT IS ALSO GREAT WITH ANY GRILLED
MEAT, CHARRED HALLOUMI OR A FRAGRANT STEW.

SERVES 4
READY IN 15 MINUTES

2 pitta breads
1 cucumber, deseeded and
    roughly chopped
½ small red onion, finely sliced
100g/3½oz/heaped ¾ cup
    pitted black olives
200g/7oz small cherry
    tomatoes, halved
1 large handful mint leaves,
    roughly chopped
1 large handful parsley leaves,
    roughly chopped

For the dressing
3 tbsp olive oil
juice of 1 lemon
¼ tsp sumac
sea salt and freshly ground black
    pepper

1 Toast the pitta bread until golden and set aside to cool.

2 Whisk together the dressing ingredients in a large mixing
bowl and season with a good pinch of salt and pepper.
Add the cucumber, onion, olives, cherry tomatoes,
mint and parsley, and toss everything together.

3 Once the pitta bread has cooled, crunch half of it between
your hands and sprinkle the pieces over the salad. Toss
everything together until well combined.

4 Transfer the salad to a large serving bowl, then break the
rest of the pitta over the top and serve immediately.

STIR-FRIES

SZECHUAN LAMB NOODLES

1 Cook the noodles according to the packet instructions. Drain, drizzle with 2 tablespoons of the oil to prevent the noodles from sticking and set aside.

2 Heat a wok over a high heat and add the remaining oil. Once the oil is smoking hot, add the peanuts, chilli flakes, Szechuan peppercorns, garlic and ginger. Stir-fry for 10 seconds until fragrant, then add the lamb and leek. Stir-fry for 3–4 minutes, or until everything turns golden brown and the lamb is beautifully tender but still a little pink in the middle.

3 Use a knife to cut through the noodles a couple of times, then tip them into the wok. Cutting the noodles will help them to mix with the other ingredients. Pour over the oyster sauce and soy sauce and mix together well until the noodles are completely coated and warmed through. Serve immediately.

SERVES 4
READY IN 15 MINUTES

250g/9oz egg noodles
4 tbsp vegetable oil
50g/1¾oz/⅓ cup unsalted peanuts
½ tsp chilli flakes
1 tsp Szechuan peppercorns
2 garlic cloves, finely chopped
2.5cm/1in piece root ginger, peeled and finely chopped
200g/7oz lamb steak or fillet, finely sliced
1 leek, finely sliced lengthways
1 tbsp oyster sauce
2 tbsp light soy sauce

BEEF CHILLI & MINT STIR-FRY

SERVES 2
READY IN 15 MINUTES

140g/5oz fine egg noodles
2½ tbsp groundnut (peanut) oil
2 garlic cloves
2.5cm/1in piece fresh root
  ginger
1 red chilli
2 sirloin steaks (about
  120g/4¼oz each)
55g/2oz/heaped ⅓ cup peanuts
1 tsp rice wine vinegar
1 tbsp light soy sauce
3 tbsp oyster sauce
150g/5½oz/1⅔ cups bean
  sprouts
1 handful of small mint leaves

NEVER ONE TO MISS A MEAL, I ORDERED MY LUNCH TO GO AS I WAS LEAVING MY HOTEL IN LAOS TO HEAD TO THE AIRPORT AND BACK TO BLIGHTY. I WAS LITERALLY EATING MY FOOD AS I WALKED TO THE TAXI. BOY, AM I GLAD THAT I AM GREEDY. LUNCH WAS SUPERB – A SIMPLE BEEF STIR-FRY WITH CHILLI, GARLIC AND A FEW PEANUTS, WHICH WAS LIFTED SOMEWHERE NEW WITH A HANDFUL OF MINT LEAVES. THE MINT WAS A SUPERB ADDITION TO A CLASSIC SOUTH-EAST ASIAN STIR-FRY AND PROBABLY EVEN WORTH MISSING A FLIGHT FOR.

1 Cook the noodles in boiling water for for 4–5 minutes until soft, or as directed on the packet. Drain in a colander and drizzle with ½ tablespoon of the oil to prevent the noodles from sticking, then leave to one side. Meanwhile, peel and finely slice the garlic and ginger. Cut the top off the chilli, then slice the chilli. Trim the fat off the beef and slice into strips about 2mm/1⁄16 in thick.

2 Heat a wok over a high heat and add 1 tablespoon of the oil. Put in the peanuts and stir-fry for 1 minute or until golden. Remove with a slotted spoon and transfer to kitchen paper to drain. Tip the oil out of the wok and return the wok to a high heat. Once smoking, add the remaining oil and the beef. Leave to sear for 40 seconds, then stir-fry for 30 seconds to take on some colour. Chuck in the garlic, ginger and chilli, and continue to stir-fry for 2–3 minutes until golden.

3 Pour in the rice wine vinegar, soy sauce and oyster sauce, and mix well. Add the bean sprouts and continue to stir-fry for 1–2 minutes until the bean sprouts are just tender but still have a little bite. Turn off the heat, then tip in the peanuts and add the mint. Give it a final mix, then add the noodles, stir and serve.

COCONUT & GINGER CHICKEN

THIS IS A SOUTH INDIAN TAKE ON A STIR-FRY WITH JUST A TINY BIT OF SAUCE TO COAT THE CHICKEN. IT'S PERFECT WITH DAL AND RICE – THEY'RE BEST MATES. I LIKE THIS DISH VERY HOT, AND USUALLY WITH DOUBLE THE AMOUNT OF CHILLI POWDER. MAKE IT WITH THE NORMAL AMOUNT TO BEGIN WITH AND SEE WHAT YOU THINK – YOU CAN ALWAYS ADD MORE AT THE END, BUT TAKING IT OUT WOULD BE A REAL TASK.

1 Put the chicken, garam masala, chilli powder and salt in a large bowl and mix until all of the chicken is well coated. Cover and set aside for 30 minutes, or overnight in the refrigerator if time allows.

2 Heat a wok over a medium heat and add the oil. When the oil is hot, add the curry leaves, onion and ginger to the wok and stir-fry for 3–4 minutes until the onion is just turning golden. Turn the heat up to high, add the chicken and stir-fry for another 3–4 minutes, or until the chicken is starting to turn golden brown.

3 Pour in the white wine vinegar and coconut milk and cook for 1–2 minutes, or until the sauce has reduced to coat the chicken in a thin layer and the chicken is cooked through and tender.

4 Finally, rub extra dried curry leaves between your hands so that they break up and scatter over the chicken. Mix well and serve immediately with rice or dal.

SERVES 4
READY IN 45 MINUTES

500g/1lb 2oz boneless, skinless chicken breasts, cut into 2cm/¾in cubes
2 tsp garam masala
1 tsp chilli powder
1 tsp sea salt
2 tbsp vegetable oil
a large pinch dried curry leaves, plus extra to serve
1 red onion, finely chopped
2.5cm/1in piece root ginger, peeled and finely chopped
1 tbsp white wine vinegar
200ml/7fl oz/scant 1 cup coconut milk
steamed rice or dal, to serve

VIETNAMESE CHILLI & LEMONGRASS CHICKEN

SERVES 4
READY IN 10 MINUTES

6 lemongrass stalks, plus extra
   stalks to serve
2 tbsp vegetable oil
4 garlic cloves, finely chopped
1 red chilli, deseeded and finely
   chopped
500g/1lb 2oz boneless, skinless
   chicken thighs, cut into bite-
   sized pieces
2 tbsp fish sauce
1 tbsp soy sauce
a pinch of sugar
1 handful coriander (cilantro)
   leaves, roughly chopped
rice noodles, to serve

1 To prepare the lemongrass, remove the really tough outer leaves and cut off the ends of the stalks. Starting at the fatter end, roughly slice each lemongrass stalk into rings. You should see a purple band in the rings. Stop slicing when there are no more purple bands and discard the rest of the lemongrass, as it will be too tough to eat. Give the lemongrass slices a quick blast in a mini food processor until they are very finely chopped.

2 Heat a wok over a high heat and add the oil. Once the oil is smoking, chuck in the lemongrass, garlic and red chilli and stir-fry for 10 seconds, or until fragrant. Add the chicken and then stir-fry for 3–4 minutes, or until the chicken is golden and cooked through.

3 Tip in the fish sauce, soy sauce and sugar and stir-fry for another 30 seconds, then chuck in the chopped coriander (cilantro). Serve immediately with rice noodles and the extra lemongrass stalks.

TAMARIND & LEMONGRASS CHICKEN

THIS SIMPLE STIR-FRY RELIES ON LEMONGRASS, GARLIC AND CHILLI TO GIVE IT A REAL PUNCH WHILE THE GROUND CORIANDER PROVIDES THE PERFECT BACKGROUND WARMTH. LIKE EVERY GREAT DISH, IT NEEDS SEASONING. THE SALT ELEMENT COMES FROM THE STRINGENT FISH SAUCE AND THE SOURNESS FROM THE BEAUTIFUL TAMARIND WATER, WHICH ALSO WORKS TO BRING ALL THE FLAVOURS TOGETHER PERFECTLY.

SERVES 4
READY IN 1 HOUR

2 lemongrass stalks
3 garlic cloves
500g/1lb 2oz boneless, skinless chicken thighs, cut into bite-sized pieces
1 tsp chilli flakes
2 tsp ground coriander
1 tsp sugar
1½ tbsp fish sauce
1 tsp tamarind paste
2 tbsp vegetable oil
1 red pepper, deseeded and cut into bite-sized pieces
1 tbsp soy sauce

1 To prepare the lemongrass, remove the really tough outer leaves and cut off the ends of the stalks. Starting at the fatter end, roughly slice each lemongrass stalk into rings. You should see a purple band in the rings. Stop slicing when there are no more purple bands and discard the rest of the lemongrass, as it will be too tough to eat. Put the lemongrass slices in a mini food processor with the garlic and grind to a smooth paste.

2 Transfer the paste to a large mixing bowl and add the chicken, chilli flakes, coriander, sugar and fish sauce. Mix until all of the chicken is well coated, then cover and leave to marinate for 30 minutes, or overnight in the refrigerator if time allows.

3 Put the tamarind paste and 100ml/3½fl oz/⅓ cup water in a small bowl and mix well. Leave to stand for 5 minutes, or until the paste has dissolved, then remove any lumps.

4 Heat the oil in a large wok over a high heat. Once smoking, add the marinated chicken and the red pepper and stir-fry for 3–4 minutes, or until the chicken is starting to turn golden brown. Pour in the tamarind water and soy sauce and stir-fry for a further 3–4 minutes, or until the chicken is cooked through and tender and the sauce has reduced right down and is beautifully sticky. Serve immediately.

CHILLI & BASIL SCALLOPS

FOR MANY YEARS MY BROTHER TOM HAS BEEN A LOYAL EATING COMPANION OF MINE, A WINGMAN, WHO LOVES HIS FOOD AND IS ALSO REAL FUN TO GO OUT WITH. ANNOYINGLY HE'S MOVED TO HONG KONG WITH HIS LOVELY WIFE RACHEL TO LIVE, WHICH MAKES DINNER A BIT HARDER TO ORGANIZE. TOM'S FIRST CHOICE WHENEVER WE DO GET TO GO OUT IS SOMETHING WITH SCALLOPS, SO THESE BEAUTIFUL, ASIAN-INSPIRED SCALLOPS ARE HERE TO KEEP HIM HAPPY. NOW ALL HE HAS TO DO IS COOK THEM FOR ME.

1 Heat the oil in a large wok over a high heat. When smoking hot, chuck in the garlic and red chillies and stir-fry for 30 seconds until fragrant. Add the onion and stir-fry for 1 minute, then tip in the scallops and stir-fry for a further 1–2 minutes, or until the scallops start to turn golden at the edges.

2 Pour in the soy sauce and fish sauce and sprinkle in the sugar and black pepper. Mix well and stir-fry for 1 minute, or until the scallops are just cooked through and tender. Throw in the basil leaves, mix well and serve immediately. You could use scallop shells, if liked.

SERVES 4
READY IN 10 MINUTES

2 tbsp vegetable oil
4 garlic cloves, finely chopped
2 red chillies, deseeded and finely chopped
1 red onion, finely sliced
500g/1lb 2oz scallops, with or without roe attached
1 tbsp light soy sauce
1 tbsp fish sauce
¼ tsp sugar
½ tsp coarsely ground black pepper
2 large handfuls basil leaves, roughly chopped

STIR-FRIED CHILLI & CORIANDER SQUID

MY FIRST NIGHT IN BANGKOK DURING MY TRAVELS WAS A DISASTER. DESPITE NOT HAVING BEEN THERE FOR TEN YEARS, I THOUGHT I KNEW THE CITY LIKE THE BACK OF MY HAND. I WANDERED ROUND, AND MUCH TO MY DISAPPOINTMENT, ATE NOTHING OF ANY MERIT, SO THE NEXT DAY I TOOK NO CHANCES AND STUCK TO WHAT I KNOW BEST – FOOD MARKETS. I WENT TO TOR KOR MARKET, IN THE NORTH OF THE CITY, WHICH WAS FULL OF HUNGRY OFFICE WORKERS LOOKING FOR LUNCH. FORGET A CHEEKY CHICKEN AND BACON SANDWICH, THIS PLACE HAD AMAZING CURRIES AND NOODLES, BRAISED PORK WITH GREEN BEANS, CLAMS IN A RED CURRY SAUCE, GRILLED SATAY, OYSTER OMELETTES, PAPAYA SALADS – AND THIS BRILLIANTLY HOT, STIR-FRIED SQUID. IF I COULD HAVE THIS DISH AS A QUICK WORKING LUNCH EVERY DAY, I WOULD BE A VERY HAPPY MAN.

SERVES 4
READY IN 10 MINUTES

700g/1lb 9oz baby squid, cleaned
2 tbsp vegetable oil
1 tsp chilli flakes
2 garlic cloves, finely chopped
2 tbsp oyster sauce
1 tbsp fish sauce
juice of ½ lime
1 large handful coriander (cilantro) leaves, roughly chopped

1 Cut the squid tentacles from the squid tube and keep whole, then cut open the tubes and score, using a sharp knife, in a criss cross pattern on the inside.

2 Heat the oil in a wok over a medium heat. When hot, add the chilli flakes and garlic, stir-fry for 30 seconds until fragrant and then add the squid. Stir-fry for 2–3 minutes, or until the squid is pale and cooked through. Pour over the oyster sauce, fish sauce and lime juice and stir-fry for 30 seconds to combine.

3 Throw in the chopped coriander (cilantro), mix well and serve immediately.

BEIJING TEA-HOUSE VEGETABLES

SERVES 4
READY IN 15 MINUTES

2 tbsp vegetable oil

1 tsp Szechuan peppercorns

3 garlic cloves, sliced
   lengthways

2.5cm/1in piece root ginger,
   peeled and finely chopped

1 red onion, finely chopped

1 tsp chilli flakes

250g/9oz oyster mushrooms,
   torn in smaller pieces

200g/7oz pak choi (bok choy),
   cut in half

2 tbsp soy sauce

1 tbsp vegetarian oyster sauce
rice, to serve (optional)

I GOT MY INSPIRATION FOR THIS DELICIOUS DISH AT A RESTAURANT CALLED HAN CANG IN THE XICHENG DISTRICT OF BEIJING, WHERE I ATE LUNCH WITH FRIENDS ONE MEMORABLE AUTUMN DAY. WE WALKED THERE VIA THE BEAUTIFUL COMPLEX OF LAKES THAT SPREAD OUT FROM THE FORBIDDEN PALACE, OVER ORNATE CHINESE BRIDGES WITH BROWN AND ORANGE LEAVES DRIFTING GENTLY UNDERNEATH AND PAST THE ROWS OF GOVERNMENT EXERCISE BIKES AND CROSS TRAINERS THAT LINE THE BANKS OF THE LAKES. AMAZING! LUNCH WAS A TASTE OF REAL CHINA. WE HAD SWEET AND SOUR FISH, BEEF HOT POT AND A LOVELY STIR-FRIED MUSHROOM DISH. THIS IS MY VERSION OF THAT STIR-FRY.

1 Heat a large wok over a high heat and add the oil. Once smoking hot, remove from the heat and add the Szechuan peppercorns. Stir in the hot oil for 30 seconds and then remove with a slotted spoon. This will give you all their spicy numbing flavour without leaving behind any gritty bits.

2 Reheat the wok over a high heat. Once smoking hot again, add the garlic, ginger, onion and chilli flakes and stir-fry for 1–2 minutes, or until everything starts to turn golden. Add the mushrooms and stir-fry for another 2 minutes until they start to wilt and take on a little colour, then add the pak choi (bok choy) and stir-fry for 2 minutes until it starts to soften. Pour in the soy sauce and oyster sauce and stir-fry for 1 minute until everything is coated in the rich juices and piping hot.

SRI LANKAN FRIED RICE

1 Put the rice into a large saucepan, cover with cold water and stir, then set aside for 5 minutes to soak. Tip the rice into a colander and give it a really good rinse under the cold tap, until the water coming out of the rice runs clear. This washes the starch out of the rice and ensures you get lovely separated grains.

2 Tip the washed rice back into the saucepan and place over a medium heat. Add the cinnamon, cloves, cardamom, turmeric, salt and 600ml/21fl oz/scant 2½ cups hot water and mix until well combined. Bring to the boil, then cover, reduce the heat to low and simmer for 10–15 minutes, or until all the water has been absorbed and the rice is almost cooked but still has a little bite. Remove from the heat and remove the saucepan lid. Place a clean tea towel over the rice, then replace the lid and set aside to steam for 5–10 minutes.

3 Meanwhile, melt the butter in a large wok over a medium heat. Once melted and hot, add the carrots and red chilli and stir-fry for 5–6 minutes, or until the carrot is soft. Add the cashew nuts and stir-fry for 1 minute, then pour over the eggs and stir-fry for a further 2–3 minutes, or until the eggs are cooked through.

4 Add the cooked rice and spring onions to the wok and mix well with a fork, fluffing up the rice as you go. Serve immediately.

SERVES 4
READY IN 40 MINUTES

350g/12oz/1¾ cups
    basmati rice
5cm/2in cinnamon stick
4 cloves
4 cardamom pods
1 tsp turmeric
1 tsp sea salt
50g/1¾oz butter
1 large carrot, grated or finely
    chopped
1 red chilli, deseeded and finely
    chopped
85g/3oz/heaped ½ cup cashew
    nuts
2 eggs, beaten
6 spring onions (scallions),
    finely sliced lengthways then
    roughly chopped

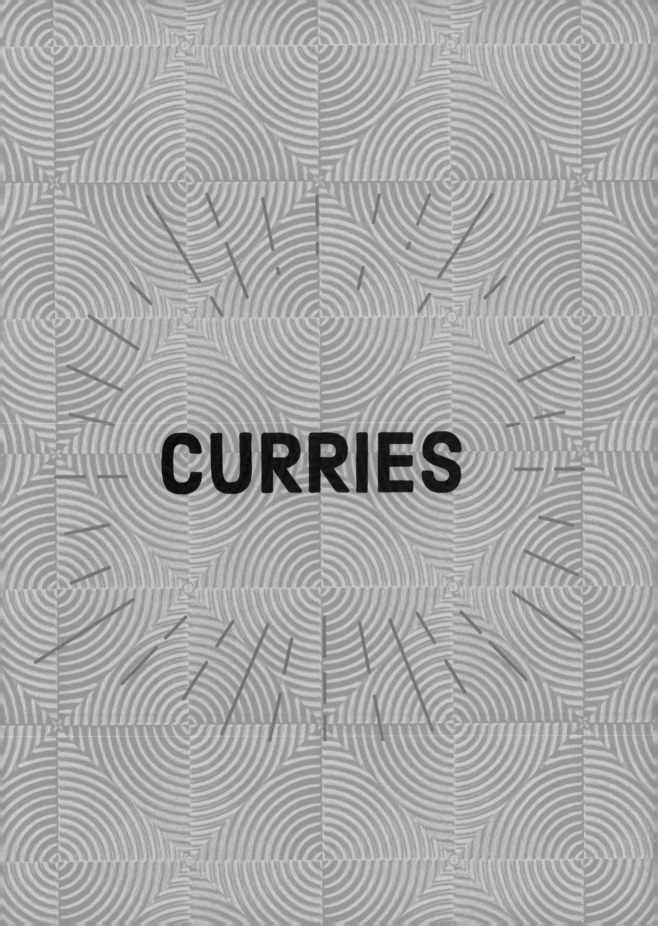

CURRIES

FOUR BROTHERS BEEF CURRY

SERVES 4
READY IN 30 MINUTES

750g/1lb 10oz new potatoes

3 lemongrass stalks

3 garlic cloves

1 red chilli

2 tbsp groundnut (peanut) oil

4 cardamom pods

2 star anise

5cm/2in cinnamon stick

4 cloves

400ml/14fl oz/generous 1½
    cups coconut cream

2 tbsp tomato purée (paste)

2 tbsp fish sauce

1 tsp sugar

4 sirloin steaks (about
    125g/4½oz each)

1 lime

1 Cut the unpeeled potatoes in half, then cook them in a large saucepan of boiling water for 10–12 minutes until tender. Drain and leave in the colander.

2 Meanwhile, remove the tough outer leaves from the lemongrass and cut off the ends of the stalks. Peel the garlic and cut the top off the chilli. Chuck the lemongrass, garlic and chilli into a mini food processor, and blend into a paste.

3 Heat the oil in a large, shallow saucepan over a medium heat and add the cardamom, star anise, cinnamon and cloves. Stir-fry for 30 seconds until fragrant, then tip in the spice paste and stir-fry for 10 seconds until it also releases its fragrance. Pour in the coconut cream and add the tomato purée (paste), fish sauce and sugar. Mix everything together really well and simmer gently.

4 Slice the steaks into strips 5cm/2in wide and add them to the pan with the sauce. Carefully tip in the potatoes and mix well. Bring to the boil, then cover, reduce the heat to low and simmer gently for 5 minutes. Remove the lid and cook for another 10 minutes, stirring occasionally, until the beef is just cooked through and the sauce is brilliantly thick.

5 While the steak cooks, cut the lime into quarters. Serve the curry with the wedges of lime to freshen it up.

GOAN CINNAMON & MINT CHICKEN

THIS CLASSIC GOAN DISH IS ONE OF MY FAVOURITE CURRIES EVER. IT'S VIBRANT IN COLOUR AND FRESH TASTING, BUT THE BEST THING IS THAT IT'S SO SIMPLE TO MAKE. BUNG EVERYTHING INTO A BLENDER TO MAKE A KILLER SAUCE, FRY THE CHICKEN, POUR OVER THE SAUCE AND COOK FOR A FEW MINUTES. WHAT COULD BE SIMPLER?

1 Cook the rice in boiling water for 10–12 minutes until soft, or as directed on the packet. Drain in a colander, then cover the rice with a clean tea towel while still in the colander, and leave to one side.

2 Meanwhile, cut the top off each chilli and roll the chilli between your hands to deseed it, then chuck them both into a blender or food processor. Peel the garlic and add it to the blender with the coriander (cilantro) leaves and stalks, mint, cinnamon, black pepper, sugar, Worcestershire sauce and a good pinch of salt. Peel and add the ginger, then squeeze in the juice from the lime and add 100ml/3½fl oz/generous ⅓ cup water. Blend into a smooth sauce.

3 Slice the chicken into thin strips. Heat the oil in a frying pan over a high heat. Add the chicken and stir-fry for 5–6 minutes until it starts to turn golden brown. Tip in the green sauce and reduce the heat to medium. Pour 100ml/3½fl oz/generous ⅓ cup water into the blender, swill it around and add it to the pan to get every last drop of flavour into the dish. Mix everything together really well and simmer for 5–6 minutes, stirring occasionally, until the chicken is cooked through and tender. Serve with the rice.

SERVES 2
READY IN 20 MINUTES

120g/4¼oz/scant ⅔ cup basmati rice
2 green chillies
3 garlic cloves
2 large handfuls of coriander (cilantro) leaves and stalks
1 large handful of mint leaves
½ tsp ground cinnamon
½ tsp freshly ground black pepper
1 tsp sugar
1½ tsp Worcestershire sauce
1cm/½in piece fresh root ginger
1 lime
300g/10½oz boneless, skinless chicken thighs
1 tbsp groundnut oil
sea salt

KERALA KORMA

SERVES 4
READY IN 30 MINUTES

500ml/17fl oz/2 cups coconut
  cream
50g/1¾oz/⅓ cup cashew nuts
2.5cm/1in piece root ginger,
  peeled
½ green chilli, deseeded
1 tsp ground coriander
½ tsp ground cumin
1½ tsp sea salt
2 tbsp vegetable oil
1 large onion, finely chopped
a large pinch of fresh curry
  leaves
500g/1lb 2oz boneless, skinless
  chicken thighs, finely sliced
juice of 1 lime
rice, to serve

I DISCOVERED THIS WONDERFUL TAKE ON THE CLASSIC KORMA IN THE HILLS OF KERALA IN SOUTH INDIA. WHEN I WAS YOUNG, MY PARENTS OFTEN FED ME AND MY SIBLINGS KORMAS, A MILD CURRY, AS A WAY OF 'BREAKING US IN' TO THE DELIGHTS OF MORE HEAVILY SPICED CURRIES. AS MY TASTE FOR ALL THINGS SPICY GREW, I LEFT THIS INTRODUCTORY CURRY BEHIND AND MOVED ON TO A NEW WORLD OF CURRIED DELIGHTS. THIS MODERN RECIPE IS DEFINITELY A REASON TO REVISIT THE KORMA. FRESH, SAVOURY AND WITH A BACKGROUND HEAT FROM THE CHILLI, IT'S A MILLION MILES AWAY FROM THE SWEET, BLAND CURRY THAT IS SERVED UP IN TOO MANY LOCAL INDIAN RESTAURANTS.

1 Put the coconut cream, cashew nuts, ginger, green chilli, coriander, cumin and salt into a food processor and blend to a smooth sauce.

2 Heat the oil in a saucepan over a medium heat, then add the onion and cook, stirring occasionally, for 6–8 minutes, or until the onion has turned golden. Pour in the coconut sauce, mix well and cook over a medium heat for 1 minute, stirring continuously, then add the curry leaves.

3 Add the chicken and lime juice and bring to the boil. Cover, reduce the heat to low and simmer for 12–15 minutes, or until the chicken is cooked through and tender and the sauce thick. If its gets too thick and gloopy, add a little hot water to loosen it up. Serve immediately with rice.

INDIAN CHICKEN & SPINACH CURRY

EVERYWHERE I WENT IN INDIA THERE WAS A DIFFERENT TAKE ON THIS CLASSIC CURRY: SOMETIMES THE MAIN INGREDIENT WAS LAMB AND SOMETIMES THE INDIAN CHEESE PANEER (THIS IS A GREAT SUBSTITUTE IF YOU'RE VEGETARIAN). FOR MY VERSION, I USE CHICKEN AND GET THE BLENDER TO DO MOST OF THE WORK, SO IT'S NICE AND EASY. IF YOU WANT A HEALTHY VERSION, LEAVE OUT THE CREAM – IT WILL STILL TASTE SUPERB.

SERVES 4
READY IN 50 MINUTES

250g/9oz baby spinach
1½ tsp garam masala
1 tsp sea salt
1 large onion, roughly chopped
2 tomatoes, quartered
4 garlic cloves
2.5cm/1in piece root ginger, peeled and roughly chopped
½ green chilli, deseeded
2 tbsp vegetable oil
2 tsp cumin seeds
500g/1lb 2oz boneless, skinless chicken thighs, cut into bite-sized pieces
60ml/2fl oz/¼ cup double cream (optional)

1 Bring a large saucepan, half-filled with water, to the boil and add the spinach. Cook for 1–2 minutes until just wilting, then strain, reserving the cooking water. Put the spinach and 100ml/3½fl oz/¹/₃ cup of the cooking water into a food processor or blender and purée until smooth. If using an upright blender, remember to leave a tiny gap in the lid for the steam to escape. Transfer the spinach to a bowl and set aside to cool.

2 Using the same food processor (don't worry about washing it), blend the garam masala, salt, onion, tomatoes, garlic, ginger, green chilli and a little water until smooth.

3 Heat the oil in a large saucepan over a medium heat and throw in the cumin seeds. Wait 10 seconds until they start crackling, then pour in the tomato mixture. Give it a good stir, cover, reduce the heat to low and simmer for 30 minutes, stirring occasionally.

4 Tip in the spinach, chicken and cream, if using, and stir well. Turn the heat up to medium-high and cook, stirring occasionally, for 12–15 minutes, or until the chicken is cooked through and tender.

KADAHI CHICKEN

I LOVE THAT A CURRY CAN BE SO FRESH, HEALTHY AND EXCITING, AND MY CHICKEN KADAHI IS PROOF THAT YOU DON'T NEED MORE THAN FIVE SPICES TO MAKE A CURRY REALLY SPECTACULAR. THE CUMIN SEEDS PROVIDE A WONDERFUL, NUTTY SPICE BASE AND THE SIMPLE FLAVOURS OF THE GARLIC, GINGER, GARAM MASALA AND TURMERIC WORK TOGETHER TO PROVIDE EVERYTHING ELSE. THE LEMON JUICE FRESHENS THE CURRY AND BRINGS OUT THE FLAVOURS OF THE SPICES EVEN MORE.

1 Heat a wok over a medium heat and add the oil. Chuck in the cumin seeds, allow them to crackle for 10 seconds, then add the onion. Stir-fry for 3–4 minutes, or until the onion starts turning golden, then add the green chilli, ginger, tomatoes, garam masala, turmeric and salt. Mix well and stir-fry for 5–6 minutes, or until the tomatoes have started to break down and form a sauce.

2 Add the chicken and green (bell) pepper, reduce the heat to low and simmer, stirring occasionally, for 12–15 minutes, or until the chicken is cooked through. Add the lemon juice and give it one last mix. Serve immediately with rice, if liked.

SERVES 4
READY IN 30 MINUTES

2 tbsp vegetable oil
2 tsp cumin seeds
1 large onion, finely chopped
1 green chilli, deseeded and finely chopped
2.5cm/1in piece root ginger, peeled and finely chopped
4 tomatoes, roughly chopped
1 tsp garam masala
½ tsp turmeric
1½ tsp salt
500g/1lb 2oz boneless, skinless chicken thighs, cut into thin strips
1 green (bell) pepper, deseeded and cut into thin strips
juice of ½ lemon
rice, to serve (optional)

CAMBODIAN SEAFOOD AMOK

1 Cook the rice noodles in boiling water for 4–5 minutes until soft, or as directed on the packet. Drain in a colander and drizzle with the oil to prevent the noodles from sticking. Cover and leave to one side.

2 Meanwhile, to make the curry paste, put all the curry paste ingredients into a mini food processor and blend into a smooth paste, adding a little water if necessary.

3 Heat a large wok over a medium heat and add the curry paste. Stir-fry for 30 seconds, or until fragrant. Pour in the coconut cream and fish sauce for the seafood curry, squeeze in the juice from the lime and mix everything together really well. Bring to the boil while you prepare the fish.

4 Chop the haddock into bite-sized pieces. Chuck them into the hot amok sauce and add the mixed seafood. Gently mix everything together, reduce the heat to low and simmer gently for 5–6 minutes, stirring occasionally, until the fish starts to flake and the seafood is cooked through.

5 Serve the curry with the rice noodles, topped with the chopped coriander (cilantro).

SERVES 2
READY IN 15 MINUTES

100g/3½oz medium rice noodles
1 tbsp groundnut (peanut) oil
250ml/9fl oz/1 cup coconut cream
1 tbsp fish sauce
½ lime
2 haddock fillets (about 150g/5½oz each)
115g/4oz prepared raw mixed seafood, such as mussels, king prawns (jumbo shrimp) and squid rings
1 small handful of coriander (cilantro) leaves, roughly chopped

For the curry paste
1cm/½in piece fresh root ginger, peeled and roughly chopped
2 lemongrass stalks, outer skin removed and roughly chopped
3 garlic cloves, peeled
½ tsp turmeric
2 dried red chillies
½ tsp freshly ground black pepper
½ tsp sugar
30g/1oz/scant ¼ cup peanuts
2 tbsp groundnut (peanut) oil

KERALAN SEAFOOD CURRY

SERVES 4
READY IN 25 MINUTES

250g/9oz/1¼ cups basmati rice
2.5cm/1in piece fresh root
    ginger, peeled
6 garlic cloves, peeled
1 green chilli, top removed
2 tsp ground coriander
½ tsp turmeric
2 tbsp groundnut (peanut) oil
2 tsp black mustard seeds
2 large pinches of dried curry
    leaves
400ml/14fl oz/generous 1½
    cups coconut milk
½ lime
250g/9oz boneless tilapia fillets
    or other white fish fillets, cut
    into bite-sized pieces
350g/12oz mixed seafood, such
    as squid rings, raw, peeled
    king prawns (jumbo shrimp),
    shelled mussels
250g/9oz/heaped 1¾ cups
    cherry tomatoes, halved
1 handful of coriander (cilantro)
    leaves
sea salt

1 Cook the rice in boiling water for 10–12 minutes until soft, or as directed on the packet. Drain and return to the pan. Cover the pan with a clean tea towel and then the lid. Leave to one side to allow the rice to fluff up.

2 Meanwhile, put the ginger, garlic chilli, ground coriander, turmeric and a good pinch of salt in a mini food processor and blend into a smooth paste, adding a little water if necessary, and leave to one side.

3 Heat the oil in a large saucepan over a medium heat and add the mustard seeds and curry leaves. Let them crackle for a few seconds, then tip in the spice paste. Stir-fry for 30 seconds, or until fragrant, then pour in the coconut milk. Squeeze in the juice from the lime and add a pinch of salt. Mix everything together really well and bring to the boil.

4 Chop the fish into large, bite-sized pieces and add to the boiling sauce. Put the seafood and cherry tomatoes into the sauce and mix gently. Bring back to the boil, cover and reduce the heat to medium-low. Cook for 6–8 minutes, stirring occasionally, until all the seafood is cooked through and tender. Scatter the coriander (cilantro) over the cooked curry and serve with the rice.

RITA'S TAMARIND & COCONUT PRAWNS

SERVES 4
READY IN 20 MINUTES

250g/9oz/1¼ cups basmati rice
2 tbsp groundnut (peanut) oil
2 onions, peeled and finley sliced
3 dried red chillies
10 peppercorns
1 tsp paprika
½ tsp turmeric
400ml/14fl oz/generous 1½ cups coconut milk
3 tsp tamarind paste
500g/1lb 2oz raw, peeled king prawns (jumbo shrimp) (with or without tails)
1 handful of coriander (cilantro) leaves, roughly chopped
sea salt

THIS IS A SUPER-QUICK PRAWN CURRY, WHICH IS HOT, SWEET AND SOUR ALL AT ONCE. IF YOU CAN'T FIND TAMARIND, JUST SQUEEZE IN THE JUICE OF A LIME. AND CHILLI POWDER AND FRESHLY GROUND BLACK PEPPER ARE FINE IF YOU DON'T HAVE THE WHOLE SPICES.

1 Cook the rice in boiling water for 10–12 minutes until soft, or as directed on the packet. Drain in a colander and return to the pan. Cover the pan with a clean tea towel and then the lid. Leave to one side so that the rice can fluff up ready to eat.

2 Meanwhile, heat the oil in a large saucepan over a medium heat and add the onions. Cook for 4–5 minutes, stirring occasionally, or until just turning golden.

3 While the onions cook, chuck the chillies and peppercorns into a spice grinder, and grind into a fine powder. Tip the ground spices into the pan with the cooked onions and add the paprika, turmeric and a good pinch of salt.

4 Mix well, pour in the coconut milk and add the tamarind paste. Mix everything together really well so that the sauce takes on a rich red colour. Bring to the boil and add the prawns (jumbo shrimp). Give them a good stir in the hot sauce, then cover and cook for 5–6 minutes, stirring occasionally, until the prawns are cooked through and beautifully pink. Scatter the coriander (cilantro) over the cooked curry and serve with the rice.

SINGAPORE LAKSA

SERVES 4
READY IN 20 MINUTES

1 tsp tamarind paste
400ml/14fl oz/1½ cups coconut milk
250g/9oz raw large king prawns (jumbo shrimp), peeled and deveined
110g/3¾oz/1¼ cups bean sprouts
110g/3¾oz rice noodles
2 tbsp vegetable oil
sea salt
4 coriander (cilantro) sprigs, to serve

For the spice paste
2 lemongrass stalks
1 red chilli
4 garlic cloves
1 tsp shrimp paste
½ tsp turmeric
2 tbsp vegetable oil

1 To prepare the spice paste, remove the really tough outer leaves of the lemongrass and cut off the ends of the stalks. Starting at the fatter end, roughly slice each lemongrass stalk into rings. You should see a purple band in the rings. Stop slicing when there are no more purple bands, as the tops will be too tough to eat. Set the tops aside to add to the laksa later and put the sliced lemongrass in a mini food processor. Add the other spice paste ingredients and blend to a smooth paste.

2 Put the tamarind paste and 100ml/3½fl oz/⅓ cup water in a small bowl. Mix well and leave to stand for 5 minutes, or until the paste has dissolved, then remove any lumps. Heat a large saucepan over a medium heat and spoon in the spice paste. Stir-fry the paste for 30 seconds until fragrant, then pour in the coconut milk, prepared tamarind, 200ml/7fl oz/scant 1 cup freshly boiled water and season with a pinch of salt. Mix well, then turn up the heat to high and bring to the boil. Add the prawns (jumbo shrimp), bean sprouts and lemongrass tops, turn the heat down to low and simmer, stirring occasionally, for 5 minutes, or until the prawns have turned pink and are cooked through. Remove the lemongrass tops.

3 Meanwhile, cook the noodles according to the packet instructions, drain and drizzle with the oil to prevent sticking. Divide the cooked noodles into four deep bowls and ladle in the hot soup. Add a coriander (cilantro) sprig to each bowl and serve immediately.

ALLEPPY PRAWN CURRY

1 To make the curry paste, put all the ingredients into a mini food processor, season with a good pinch of salt and grind to a smooth paste.

2 Heat the oil in a large frying pan or skillet over a medium heat, then throw in the mustard seeds. When they start popping after about 30 seconds, add the curry paste and stir-fry for a further 30 seconds until fragrant.

3 Pour in the coconut cream and lemon juice and bring to the boil. Reduce the heat to low and simmer, stirring occasionally, for 10 minutes, or until the sauce has reduced and is really thick.

4 Add the prawns (jumbo shrimp) and simmer, stirring frequently so they cook evenly, for 5 minutes, or until the prawns have turned pink and are cooked through. Rub the dried curry leaves between your hands so that they break up and scatter over the curry. Mix well and serve immediately with rice.

SERVES 4
READY IN 20 MINUTES

2 tbsp vegetable oil
2 tsp mustard seeds
500ml/17fl oz/2 cups coconut
    cream
juice of 1 lemon
500g/1lb 2oz raw large king
    prawns (jumbo shrimp),
    peeled and deveined
a large pinch of dried curry
    leaves
rice, to serve

For the curry paste
1 green chilli, deseeded
1 red onion, roughly chopped
5cm/2in piece root ginger,
    peeled and roughly chopped
½ tsp turmeric
sea salt

MALAY YELLOW MUSSEL CURRY

SERVES 4
READY IN 20 MINUTES

2 tbsp vegetable oil
400ml/14fl oz/1½ cups
    coconut milk
juice of ½ lemon
1kg/2lb 4oz mussels, cleaned
    and beards removed
1 large handful coriander
    (cilantro) leaves

For the curry paste
2 lemongrass stalks
2.5cm/1in piece root ginger,
    peeled
2 garlic cloves
50g/1¾oz/⅓ cup unsalted
    cashew nuts
½ tsp shrimp paste
½ tsp chilli flakes
½ tsp turmeric

1 To prepare the curry paste, remove the really tough outer leaves from the lemongrass and cut off the ends of the stalks. Starting at the fatter end, roughly slice each lemongrass stalk into rings. You should see a purple band in the rings. Stop slicing when there are no more purple bands and discard the rest of the lemongrass, as it will be too tough to eat. Put the lemongrass slices in a mini food processor with the other curry paste ingredients and blend to a smooth paste.

2 Heat the oil in a large wok over a medium heat. Add the curry paste and stir-fry for 30 seconds until fragrant, then pour in the coconut milk and lemon juice. Mix well and bring to the boil, then turn the heat down to low and simmer, stirring occasionally, for 5 minutes.

3 Discard any open mussels that do not snap shut when tapped. Carefully add the mussels to the coconut mixture, then cover and cook, shaking the pan occasionally, for 5–6 minutes, or until nearly all of the mussel shells have opened.

4 Remove the mussels from the heat and divide the mussels into four bowls, discarding any mussels that are still closed. Scatter over the coriander leaves and serve immediately.

PANJIM CLAMS WITH COCONUT OKRA

1 Preheat the oven to 180°C/350°F/Gas 4. Heat the oil in a saucepan over a medium heat and add the onion and chilli. Stir-fry for 4–5 minutes until just turning golden.

2 Add the garam masala and turmeric, mix well and pour in the coconut cream. Squeeze in the juice from the lime and add a good pinch of salt. Mix well, reduce the heat to low and simmer gently, stirring occasionally, while you start the okra.

3 To make the coconut okra, split the cardamom pods open by pressing down on them with the side of a knife and set aside. Heat the oil in a wok over a high heat and add the onion, garlic, chilli, cardamom and peppercorns. Stir-fry for 2–3 minutes until just golden, then add the okra and a good pinch of salt. Stir-fry for 2 minutes, then pour in the coconut cream. Add the curry leaves to the wok by rubbing them between your hands. Mix well, cover and reduce the heat to low. Cook for 5 minutes.

4 Meanwhile, pop the naan into the oven and switch it off, so that they just warm through. Add the raisins and lime juice to the half-cooked okra, mix well, then cover and cook for 5 minutes, or until the okra is tender. While the okra finishes cooking, chuck the clams into the hot sauce, cover and cook for 4–5 minutes, shaking the pan occasionally, until the clams have opened. Discard any that remain closed. Chop the coriander (cilantro) and scatter it over the clams. Serve with the okra and naan alongside.

SERVES 4
READY IN 30 MINUTES

2 tbsp groundnut (peanut) oil
1 onion, peeled and finely chopped
1 green chilli, finely chopped
2 tsp garam masala
1 tsp turmeric
400ml/14fl oz/generous 1½ cups coconut cream
½ lime
1kg/2lb 4oz picked and cleaned clams
1 small handful of coriander (cilantro) leaves
sea salt
4 small naan breads, to serve

For the coconut okra
2 cardamom pods
2 tbsp groundnut (peanut) oil
1 red onion, peeled and finely chopped
3 garlic cloves, peeled and finely chopped
1 green chilli, finely chopped
8 black peppercorns
350g/12oz okra, tops removed
185ml/6fl oz/¾ cup coconut cream
1 large pinch of dried curry leaves
20g/¾oz/scant ¼ cup raisins
juice of ½ lime

AMISH'S GUJARATI VEGETABLE CURRY

THIS MAGNIFICENT CURRY CAN BE MADE WELL IN ADVANCE.
SIMPLY MAKE THE SAUCE AND COOK IT WITHOUT ADDING ANY
OF THE VEGETABLES. COOK THE VEGETABLES, THEN REFRESH
THEM UNDER COLD WATER. WHEN YOU WANT TO EAT, REHEAT
THE SAUCE AND ADD THE VEGETABLES. COOK UNTIL THE VEG
HAVE WARMED THROUGH, THEN SERVE.

SERVES 4
READY IN 35 MINUTES

250g/9oz/1¼ cups basmati rice
400g/14oz/scant 2 cups tinned
    chickpeas
1 onion, peeled and finely
    chopped
2 tbsp groundnut (peanut) oil
2.5cm/1in piece fresh root
    ginger
6 garlic cloves
4 tomatoes
85g/3oz/heaped ½ cup
    cashew nuts
2 tsp ground coriander
1 tsp ground cumin
1 tsp garam masala
½ tsp chilli powder
½ tsp turmeric
400g/14oz new potatoes
3 carrots
1 small cauliflower
200g/7oz green beans
1 handful of coriander leaves
sea salt

1 Cook the rice in boiling water for 10–12 minutes until soft, or as directed on the packet. Drain and rinse the chickpeas in a colander. In the same colander, drain the rice then tip the rice and chickpeas back into the pan. Cover the pan with a clean tea towel and then the lid. Leave to one side so that the rice can fluff up ready to eat.

2 Meanwhile, peel and finely chop the onion. Heat the oil in a large saucepan over a medium heat and add the onion. Cook for 4–5 minutes, stirring occasionally, until golden.

3 Peel the ginger and garlic, then chuck both into a blender or food processor with the tomatoes, 55g/2oz/heaped ⅓ cup of the cashew nuts, the ground coriander, cumin, garam masala, chilli powder, turmeric and a good pinch of salt. Blend until smooth. Pour this mixture over the cooked onion, mix well and bring to the boil. Cover, reduce the heat to low and simmer for 20 minutes, stirring occasionally.

4 Cut the potatoes into quarters while the sauce cooks. Cook them in a saucepan of boiling water for 8 minutes. Peel the carrots, then cut them, with the cauliflower, into small pieces. Cut the beans in half. Add the vegetables to the potatoes and cook for 5–6 minutes until tender, then drain. Roughly chop the coriander. Mix the vegetables into the sauce. Serve the curry and rice, sprinkled with coriander and cashew nuts.

SESAME AUBERGINES WITH KERALAN SPINACH & SWEETCORN SALAD

SERVES 4
READY IN 45 MINUTES

1 tbsp ground coriander
1 tbsp sesame seeds
½ tsp chilli powder
½ tbsp ground cumin
1½ tsp sea salt
350g/12oz baby aubergines
  (eggplants)
2 tbsp groundnut (peanut) oil
1 large red onion, peeled and
  finely chopped
2.5cm/1in piece root ginger,
  peeled and finely chopped
4 garlic cloves, peeled and finely
  chopped
3 tomatoes, finely chopped
a pinch of sugar
1 handful of coriander (cilantro)
  leaves, roughly chopped
½ lemon
250g/9oz/1¼ cups basmati rice

For the salad
1 tbsp groundnut (peanut) oil
1 tsp cumin seeds
85g/3oz/½ cup cashew nuts
225g/8oz spinach
1 red onion, peeled and finely
  chopped
juice of 1 lemon
½ red chilli, finely chopped
140g/5oz/heaped ⅔ cup tinned
  sweetcorn, drained
25g/1oz creamed coconut
sea salt

1 Put the ground coriander, sesame seeds, chilli powder, ground cumin and salt into a spice grinder, and grind into a fine powder. Remove the stalks from the baby aubergines (eggplants) and cut a 2.5cm/1in deep slit into the opposite end. Rub about half of the spices into the slits.

2 Heat the oil in a saucepan over a medium heat and chuck in the onion. Cook for 4–5 minutes, stirring occasionally, until golden. Add the ginger, garlic and tomatoes to the pan and mix well. Add the remaining ground spices, the sugar and the prepared aubergines. Mix together, then cover and simmer for 20 minutes to allow the aubergines to cook through.

3 Meanwhile, cook the rice in boiling water for 10–12 minutes until soft, or as directed on the packet. Drain and return to the pan. Cover the pan with a clean tea towel and then the lid. Leave to one side so that the rice can fluff up.

4 Make the salad while the rice cooks. Heat the oil in a wok over a medium heat and add the cumin seeds and cashew nuts. Stir-fry for 45 seconds, then add the spinach and a pinch of salt. Continue to stir-fry for 2–3 minutes until the spinach has wilted. Remove from the heat and leave to one side.

5 Put the onion in a mixing bowl, pour over the lemon juice, add the chilli, sweetcorn and a pinch of salt, then mix well. Add the cooked spinach, making sure you scrape all the oil and cumin into the mixing bowl. Mix everything together really well and transfer to a serving bowl. Grate the coconut over the top, then cover and leave to one side.

6 When the aubergines have cooked, remove the lid from the pan and cook for 5 minutes, stirring occasionally, to allow the sauce to thicken. Scatter the coriander over the cooked curry and squeeze over the juice from the lemon. Serve with the cooked rice and the colourful salad.

CHANA MASALA

FOR MOST PEOPLE, DELHI IS A PLACE TO LAND AND LEAVE: IT'S HOT, BUSY AND FULL ON. HOWEVER, MY FRIEND AYESHA ARRANGED FOR ME TO STAY WITH HER FATHER IN NEW DELHI AND MY EXPERIENCE WAS SOMEWHAT DIFFERENT. I WAS GREETED AT THE AIRPORT BY A SMART DRIVER WITH AN EVEN SMARTER MERC AND DRIVEN TO AYESHA'S FAMILY HOME – FANTASTIC! THERE WERE THREE CHEFS, AND I SPENT EVERY WAKING HOUR IN THE KITCHEN. THE FOOD WAS OUTSTANDING, AND THIS CHICKPEA DISH IS MY VERSION OF SOMETHING ONE OF THE CHEFS COOKED FOR ME.

SERVES 4
READY IN 20 MINUTES

2 tbsp vegetable oil
2 tsp cumin seeds
½ tsp sea salt
1 tsp ground coriander
½ tsp garam masala
½ tsp freshly ground black pepper
1 green chilli, deseeded and finely sliced
800g/1lb 12oz tinned chickpeas, drained and rinsed
juice of 1 lemon, plus extra wedges to serve
½ red onion, finely sliced
1 handful coriander (cilantro) leaves, chopped
good-quality olive oil, to serve

1 Heat the vegetable oil in a large pan over a medium heat, then add the cumin seeds. Let them crackle for 10 seconds, then chuck in the salt, ground coriander, garam masala, black pepper and half the green chilli. Fry, stirring constantly, for a couple of seconds until fragrant.

2 Add the chickpeas, lemon juice and about 250ml/9fl oz/1 cup freshly boiled water, which should be enough to just cover everything. Gently mash some of the chickpeas with the back of a spoon to help the sauce thicken. Turn the heat up to high, bring to the boil and cook, stirring occasionally, for 10–12 minutes until the sauce has reduced right down and is very thick and just coating the chickpeas.

3 Throw in the onion, chopped coriander (cilantro) and the remaining green chilli. This will give the dish a lovely fresh flavour and raw crunch. Mix everything together, drizzle over some olive oil and serve with wedges of lemon to squeeze over. This dish is also really delicious served chilled.

GOBI MASALA

SERVES 4
READY IN 30 MINUTES

2 tbsp vegetable oil
1 large onion, finely chopped
2.5cm /2in piece root ginger,
  peeled
  and cut into matchsticks
2 tomatoes, finely chopped
450g/1lb cauliflower florets, cut
  into bite-sized pieces
½ tsp chilli powder
1 tsp garam masala
1 tsp sea salt
1 large handful coriander
  (cilantro) leaves,
  roughly chopped
naan bread, to serve

THE REASON THIS CAULIFLOWER DISH WORKS SO WELL IS BECAUSE IT RELIES ONLY ON A FEW SIMPLE INGREDIENTS. THE ONION, TOMATO AND GINGER PROVIDE THE BASE FOR THE WHOLE DISH AND THE CAULIFLOWER THE MAIN FLAVOUR. A LITTLE CHILLI POWDER AND GARAM MASALA IS ALL IT TAKES TO GIVE A LOVELY, SPICY TASTE, WHILE THE FRESH CORIANDER (CILANTRO) LIVENS THINGS UP AT THE END. GOBI MASALA IS DELICIOUS ON ITS OWN AS WELL AS PART OF A LARGER MEAL WITH LOTS OF OTHER AMAZING DISHES.

1 Heat the oil in a large frying pan or skillet over a high heat. Add the onion and stir-fry for 3–4 minutes until golden, then add the ginger and tomatoes and stir-fry for a further 1 minute.

2 Add the cauliflower, chilli powder, garam masala, salt and 100ml/3½fl oz/⅓ cup hot water and mix well. Bring to the boil then cover, reduce the heat to low and simmer for 20–25 minutes, or until the cauliflower is tender but still has a little bite. Throw in the coriander (cilantro), mix well and serve immediately with naan bread.

RANA'S KEEMA SHEPHERD'S PIE

SERVES 4
READY IN 45 MINUTES

750g/1lb 10oz new potatoes
2 tbsp groundnut (peanut) oil
1 red onion, peeled and finely
    chopped
3 cardamom pods
3 large blades of mace
500g/1lb 2oz minced (ground)
    lamb
2.5cm/1in piece fresh root
    ginger, peeled
4 garlic cloves, peeled
100g/3½oz/heaped ⅓ cup
    tomato purée (paste)
2½ tsp garam masala
1 tsp chilli powder
½ tsp ground cinnamon
150g/5½oz/scant 1 cup frozen
    peas
30g/1oz butter
3 spring onions (scallions),
    trimmed and finely chopped
1 handful of coriander (cilantro)
    leaves
1 tbsp olive oil
sea salt

1 Cook the unpeeled potatoes in a large pan of boiling water for 15 minutes, or until tender.

2 Meanwhile, heat the groundnut (peanut) oil in a large frying pan or skillet over a medium heat and add the onion, cardamom pods and mace. Mix well, then add the lamb. Increase the heat to high and stir-fry for 3–4 minutes until the lamb is just cooked through. Reduce the heat to medium and cook for a few minutes, stirring occasionally, while you make the sauce.

3 To make the sauce, place the ginger and garlic into a mini food processor or blender, and add the tomato purée (paste), chilli powder, cinnamon, 1½ teaspoons of the garam masala and a good pinch of salt. Blend until smooth. Scoop the sauce into the pan with the lamb and add 150ml/5fl oz/scant ⅔ cup hot water and the peas. Mix well and cover, then reduce the heat to low and simmer gently for 15 minutes, stirring occasionally.

4 Drain the cooked potatoes, then return them to the pan. Mash lightly, so that they start to break up, then add the butter, remaining garam masala and a good pinch of salt. Put the lid on the saucepan until the butter has melted, then chuck the spring onions (scallions) into the pan and mix everything together well. Cover and leave to one side.

5 Preheat the grill (broiler) to high, then scatter the coriander (cilantro) over the lamb and mix well. Carefully tip the cooked mince into an ovenproof dish and spoon over the spiced potatoes. Drizzle the olive oil over the top and grill (broil) for 5 minutes, or until crisped up and golden. Serve.

GRILLS

PAPRIKA & FENNEL PORK CHOPS WITH LENTILS & BEETROOT SALAD

1 Preheat the grill (broiler) to high. Lightly crush the fennel seeds using a mortar and pestle or a spice grinder. Tip them into a mixing bowl and add the paprika and a good pinch of salt. Put the pork into a separate mixing bowl and pour over the olive oil. Mix well.

2 Transfer the pork to a grill rack and rub the spice mix over the top of the chops to completely coat them in a crust of fantastic spice. Grill (broil) the chops for 6–8 minutes on each side until golden and cooked through.

3 While the pork cooks, heat the oil in a frying pan over a medium heat and add the chorizo and garlic. Cook for 3–4 minutes, stirring occasionally, until the chorizo turns golden. Drain and rinse the lentils, then tip them into the pan with the cooked chorizo. Add the sun-dried tomato (pureé) paste, 125ml/4fl oz/½ cup boiling water and season with a pinch of salt and pepper. Mix well, reduce the heat to low and simmer gently, stirring occasionally, while you make the salad.

4 Tip the beetroot (beet) into a mixing bowl and squeeze over the juice from the orange, pour in the oil and add a pinch of salt and pepper. Mix well and tip out on to a serving plate. Scatter the rocket (arugula) over the beetroot and crumble the goat's cheese over the top. Deseed and finely chop the chilli, then sprinkle it over the salad. Cover and leave to one side.

5 Finely chop the parsley for the lentils and add it to the pan with the warmed lentils. Turn the heat up to high, mix well and cook for 1–2 minutes, stirring continuously, until thick. Serve the pork chops, spice-side up, with the lentils and the salad at the table.

SERVES 4
READY IN 30 MINUTES

1 tbsp fennel seeds
2 tsp smoked paprika
4 pork chops (about 200g/7oz each)
2 tbsp olive oil

For the lentils
1 tbsp olive oil
115g/4oz chorizo, in one piece, finely chopped
2 garlic cloves, peeled and finely chopped
400g/14oz/1½ cups tinned green lentils
2 tbsp sun-dried tomato purée (paste)
1 handful of parsley leaves
sea salt and freshly ground black pepper

For the beetroot (beet) and goat's cheese salad
200g/7oz cooked, peeled beetroot (beet), chopped into small pieces
juice from ½ orange
1 tbsp olive oil
1 handful of rocket (arugula) leaves
55g/2oz soft goat's cheese
¼ red chilli

MR WONG'S HUNAN LAMB

2 dried red chillies

1 tsp Sichuan pepper

1cm/½in piece fresh root ginger, peeled

5 spring onions (scallions), trimmed

3 tbsp groundnut (peanut) oil

6 lamb cutlets (about 500g/1lb 2oz total weight)

200g/7oz pak choi (bok choy)

1 tbsp soy sauce

juice of ½ orange

sea salt

THIS DISH IS ALL ABOUT THE BIG SPICES OF HUNANESE COOKING. A FIERY PASTE MADE FROM DRIED CHILLIES, SICHUAN PEPPER, GINGER AND SPRING ONIONS (SCALLIONS) COATS THE DELICATE LAMB CUTLETS AND TURNS THEM INTO SOMETHING FIERCE. THE SWEETNESS OF THE LAMB HANDLES ALL THE BIG FLAVOURS, AND THE DELICATE PAK CHOI, SOY AND ORANGE STIR-FRY ABSORBS SOME OF THE HEAT.

1 Preheat the grill (broiler) to high. Put the chillies, Sichuan pepper and a pinch of salt into a mini food processor, and blend into a coarse powder. Add the ginger, spring onions (scallions) and 2 tablespoons of the oil to the food processor and blend into a rough paste.

2 Lightly score both sides of the lamb cutlets in a crisscross pattern and put them in a mixing bowl. Tip in the spice paste and mix everything together really well so that the paste completely covers the lamb. Put the lamb on a grill rack and grill (broil) for 5–6 minutes on each side until golden on the outside and pink and juicy in the centre.

3 While the lamb cooks, cut the pak choi (bok choy) lengthways into quarters. Heat a wok over a high heat until smoking and pour in the remaining tablespoon of oil. Chuck in the pak choi and stir-fry for 2 minutes, then add the soy sauce and orange juice. Continue to stir-fry for 30 seconds, then reduce the heat to low and cook for 3–4 minutes until tender. Serve the stir-fry with the lamb.

KASHMIRI LAMB CUTLETS WITH PINEAPPLE SALAD & LIME RAITA

1 Preheat the grill (broiler) to high and the oven to 180°C/350°F/Gas 4. Put the Kashmiri chillies, cloves, peppercorns, cinnamon, salt and sugar in a spice grinder, and grind to a powder. Add the ginger and garlic with the white wine vinegar and oil, then blend into a smooth paste.

2 Put the lamb cutlets in a mixing bowl and tip in the spice paste. Mix everything together really well so that all the lamb is completely coated. Put the lamb on to a grill rack and grill (broil) for 6–8 minutes on each side until golden on the outside and pink and juicy in the centre.

3 While the lamb cooks, pop the flatbreads into the hot oven and turn it off, so that they warm through and don't burn. Next, make the salad. Put the chilli in a large mixing bowl. Cut the top and bottom off the pineapple, then stand it upright on your chopping board. Slice off the skin, cutting downwards from top to bottom. Cut out any pieces of skin left on the fruit. Cut the pineapple half in half lengthways, then slice off the woody core so that you are left with the soft flesh.

4 Chop the pineapple flesh into small chunks and add them to the bowl with the tomatoes, bean sprouts, grated carrot and olives. Chuck the mint leaves into the bowl with the salad, then pour over the lime juice and oil, and season with salt. Mix everything together really well.

5 To make the raita, tip the yogurt into a serving bowl, squeeze in the juice from the lime and season with a pinch of salt. Finely chop the mint and add it to the bowl. Mix well, drizzle with the oil and top with a pinch of chilli powder. Serve the cooked lamb with the creamed coconut grated over the top and the vibrant salad, raita and warm flatbreads at the table.

SERVES 4
READY IN 30 MINUTES

For the lamb cutlets
4 dried Kashmiri chillies
8 cloves
10 black peppercorns
2.5cm/1in cinnamon stick
1 tsp sea salt
1 tsp sugar
2.5cm/1in piece fresh root ginger, peeled
4 garlic cloves, peeled
2 tbsp white wine vinegar
2 tbsp olive oil
8 lamb cutlets
25g/1oz creamed coconut
4 flatbreads, to serve

For the pineapple and chilli salad
1 red chilli, deseeded and finely chopped
½ pineapple
150g/5½oz/1 cup cherry tomatoes, halved
1 carrot, peeled and grated
100g/3½oz/1 cup bean sprouts
30g/1oz/¼ cup pitted black olives
1 handful of mint leaves
1 lime
2 tbsp olive oil
sea salt

For the mint and lime raita
250g/9oz/1 cup yogurt
½ lime
1 handful of mint leaves
1 tbsp olive oil
a pinch of chilli powder

LAMB WITH TARATOR SAUCE, MASH & TOMATO SALAD

SERVES 4
READY IN 40 MINUTES

750g/1lb 10oz new potatoes
30g/1oz butter
8 small lamb chops (about
   90g/3¼oz each)
2 tsp ground allspice
2 tsp dried oregano
1 tbsp olive oil
sea salt and freshly ground black
   pepper

For the tarator sauce
1 slice of white bread
1 garlic clove, peeled
juice of 1 lemon
55g/2oz/heaped ⅓ cup pine
   nuts
1½ tsp ground cumin
55ml/1¾fl oz/scant ¼ cup olive
   oil

For the tomato and radish salad
250g/9oz/heaped 1¾ cups
   cherry tomatoes, halved
200g/7oz radishes, halved
2 spring onions (scallions),
   trimmed and finely chopped
1 handful of mint leaves,
   chopped if large
1 handful of parsley leaves
juice of 1 lemon
2 tbsp olive oil

1 Preheat the oven to 200°C/400°F/Gas 6. To make the mash, cook the unpeeled potatoes in a large saucepan of boiling water for 15 minutes, or until tender. Drain, return them to the pan, then add the butter and a good pinch of salt and pepper. Mash together until fairly smooth, then cover and keep warm.

2 Meanwhile, make the tarator sauce. Rip the bread into small pieces and put it into a food processor with the garlic, lemon juice, pine nuts, cumin and a good pinch of salt and pepper. Add 3 tablespoons water and the oil, then blend into a coarse sauce. Scoop the tarator sauce into a serving bowl, add a grinding of pepper, then cover and leave to one side.

3 Lay the lamb chops on a chopping board and gently score both sides with a sharp knife. Put the lamb in a mixing bowl and add the allspice, oregano, oil and a good pinch of salt and pepper. Mix well so that the lamb is completely coated. Put the lamb on to a grill rack over a roasting tin and roast for 8–10 minutes until tender and juicy.

4 Make the salad while the lamb cooks. Put the cherry tomatoes, radishes, spring onions (scallions), fresh herbs, lemon juice and olive oil in a serving bowl and season with a good pinch of salt and pepper. Toss together well and leave to one side. Serve the cooked lamb and mash with the salad and tarator sauce.

LEMONGRASS & LIME LAMB CHOPS WITH A SPICY MANGO SALSA

1 Put the black pepper and garlic into a mini food processor and blend into a rough paste, then transfer it to a large mixing bowl.

2 Bash the fat ends of the lemongrass stalks a couple of times with a heavy spoon to help release their delicious flavour, and add to the mixing bowl with the pepper and garlic paste. Add the oyster sauce, soy sauce and oil to the bowl. Squeeze over the lime juice and then mix until well combined. Reserve the lime halves for roasting. Drop in the lamb chops and mix until they are well coated. Cover the bowl and leave to marinate at room temperature for 30 minutes, or overnight in the refrigerator if time allows.

3 Meanwhile, gently mix the salsa ingredients together in a bowl until well combined and set aside.

4 Preheat the oven to 200°C/400°F/Gas 6. Put the chops and marinade and reserved lime halves in a shallow roasting tray and then pour the marinade over the top. Bake in the preheated oven for 12–15 minutes, or until they are brown on the outside but still pink in the middle.

5 Serve with a spoonful of the cooking juices poured over, a scattering of red chilli and coriander (cilantro) leaves and a good dollop of the salsa.

SERVES 4
READY IN 1 HOUR

1½ tbsp freshly ground black
   pepper
4 garlic cloves
2 lemongrass stalks
125ml/4fl oz/½ cup oyster
   sauce
3 tbsp light soy sauce
1 lime, halved
2 tbsp vegetable oil
8 lamb chops
½ red chilli, deseeded and finely
   sliced, to serve
1 small handful coriander
   (cilantro) leaves,
   to serve

For the salsa
1 large mango, peeled, pitted
   and finely diced
1 red chilli, deseeded and finely
   chopped
a large bunch coriander
   (cilantro) leaves,
   finely chopped
juice of 2 limes

GRILLED LAMB SKEWERS WITH BULGUR WHEAT

1 Put the red chilli and garlic in a mini food processor with a good pinch of salt and grind to a smooth paste. Add the cumin, coriander, cinnamon and olive oil and blend until lovely and smooth. Transfer to a large mixing bowl, add the lamb and mix everything together until all the meat is well coated. Cover with cling film (plastic wrap) and set aside to marinate for 30 minutes, or overnight in the refrigerator if time allows.

2 Soak four wooden skewers in water for 30 minutes. This will stop them from burning under the grill (broiler) later.

3 To make the bulgur wheat salad, cook the bulgar wheat in a saucepan of boiling water for 8–10 minutes, or until tender but still with just a little bite. Transfer to a sieve, rinse with cold water and drain, squeezing out any excess water with your hands. Tip into a mixing bowl and add the sun-dried tomatoes, onion, red chilli, dill, parsley, lemon juice and oil and season with a really good pinch of salt and pepper. Toss everything together until all the ingredients are well combined.

4 Preheat the grill (broiler) to high. Divide the lamb into four portions and push onto the four pre-soaked skewers. Place under a hot grill for 3–4 minutes on each side, or until the lamb is golden brown on the outside and pink and juicy in the middle. Serve hot with the bulgur salad, a dollop of natural yogurt, an extra grind of pepper and a scattering of dill sprigs.

SERVES 4
READY IN 45 MINUTES

1 red chilli, deseeded
4 garlic cloves, peeled
2 tsp ground cumin
2 tsp ground coriander
½ tsp ground cinnamon
4 tbsp olive oil
800g/1lb 12oz boned, trimmed, lamb leg, cut into 2.5cm/1in cubes
sea salt and freshly ground black pepper
natural yogurt, to serve

For the bulgur wheat salad
190g/6¾oz/1½ cups bulgur wheat
100g/3½oz/1 cup sun-dried tomatoes, roughly chopped
½ red onion, finely chopped
1 red chilli, deseeded and finely chopped
1 handful dill leaves, finely chopped, plus extra sprigs to serve
1 large handful parsley leaves, finely chopped
juice of ½ lemon
2 tbsp olive oil

KOREAN KEBABS

SERVES 2
READY IN 10 MINUTES

175g/6oz fillet steak

1 garlic clove, peeled and
crushed

1½ tbsp soy sauce

2 tsp clear honey

½ tsp freshly ground black
pepper

1 tsp sesame oil

½ tsp groundnut (peanut) oil

1 tsp sesame seeds

AS I ROAMED THE HIGH-TECH STREETS OF SEOUL IN KOREA,
I FOUND LITTLE FOOD STALLS NESTLED IN THE SIDE STREETS
OFFERING THE TASTIEST SNACKS. MY FAVOURITES WERE
THESE BEEF KEBABS, WHICH WERE BARBECUED OVER HOT
COALS AND SERVED WITH A BRUSHING OF STICKY MARINADE
AND CRUNCHY SESAME SEEDS. WHAT IS GREAT ABOUT THEM
IS THAT THEY ARE SO QUICK AND EASY TO MAKE YET THEY
TASTE OUT OF THIS WORLD.

1 Cut the steak into long, thin strips, about 2mm/¹⁄₁₆ in thick,
and put them in a mixing bowl.

2 Heat a griddle over a high heat until smoking. Meanwhile,
add the garlic, soy sauce, honey, black pepper, sesame oil
and groundnut (peanut) oil to the bowl with the steak. Mix
well to coat, then thread the strips of steak on to six metal
skewers.

3 Griddle the kebabs for 1–1½ minutes on each side until
charred but still pink and juicy in the centre. Transfer the
kebabs to a serving dish, scatter over the sesame seeds
and serve.

CIYA SHISH KEBABS

SERVES 4
READY IN 25 MINUTES

400g/14oz minced (ground)
    beef
1 tsp ground cumin
2 tbsp olive oil, plus extra for
    brushing
250ml/9fl oz/1 cup natural
    yogurt
4 flour tortillas
50g/1¾oz/½ cup roughly
    chopped walnuts
125g/4½oz fresh mozzarella,
    drained and roughly sliced
1 handful parsley leaves, finely
    chopped
1 handful mint leaves, finely
    chopped
4 spring onions (scallions),
    finely sliced
1 tsp sumac, plus extra to serve
lemon wedges, to serve
sea salt and freshly ground black
    pepper

THESE KEBABS ARE COMPLETELY DELICIOUS – JUICY MEAT
WITH CRUNCHY NUTS, OOZING CHEESE, LOVELY SOUR SUMAC,
LOADS OF FRESH HERBS AND CRISPY TORTILLA BREAD.
TRADITIONALLY, THE KEBABS ARE COOKED OVER CHARCOAL
USING HUGE METAL SKEWERS, BUT I JUST USE A PAIR OF
TONGS TO TURN THE MEAT UNDER THE GRILL. FEEL FREE
TO USE A SKEWER IF YOU LIKE.

1 Preheat the grill (broiler) to high. In a large mixing bowl, season the minced (ground) beef with a really good pinch of salt and pepper, add the cumin and mix well. Divide the seasoned minced beef into eight, roll out into 14cm/5½in-long sausage shapes and brush with a little oil. Place the kebabs under the hot grill and cook for 3–4 minutes on each side, or until they are just turning golden brown and are cooked through and tender.

2 Place a tablespoon of yogurt in the middle of each tortilla and spread out with the back of a spoon. Sprinkle a quarter of the walnuts, mozzarella, parsley, mint and spring onions (scallions) over each tortilla, then sprinkle each with a pinch of sumac, salt and pepper. Place two cooked kebabs on top and roll the tortilla up tightly, tucking in the side as you go.

3 Heat the oil in a frying pan or skillet over a medium heat, then fry the kebabs for 1 minute on each side, or until they turn golden brown and crispy. Slice the kebabs in half and serve immediately with the remaining yogurt, sprinkled with sumac, and lemon wedges for squeezing.

KOREAN STEAKS WITH CARROT KIMCHI & SANJIM

SERVES 4
READY IN 40 MINUTES

2 tbsp olive oil
4 rib-eye steaks (about
    250g/9oz each)
sea salt and freshly ground black
    pepper

For the carrot kimchi
1kg/2lb 4oz carrots, peeled
    and grated
4 tbsp salt
2.5cm/1in piece fresh root
    ginger, peeled and grated
1 garlic clove, peeled and
    crushed
1 tbsp fish sauce
2 tsp sugar
1 tsp chilli powder
3 tbsp yogurt
½ tsp clear honey
2 handfuls of chives, finely
    chopped

For the sanjim
1 garlic clove, peeled
12 spring onions, trimmed
60g/2¼oz/½ cup walnuts
1 tbsp light soy sauce
2 tbsp chilli sauce
2 tsp clear honey
2 tsp sesame oil

1 To make the kimchi, put the grated carrots in a large mixing bowl with the salt and pour in 750ml/26fl oz/3 cups boiling water. Mix with a wooden spoon and leave to one side for 20 minutes. Meanwhile, make the dressing for the kimchi. Mix together the ginger, garlic, fish sauce, sugar, chilli powder, yogurt and honey in a small bowl. Finely chop the chives and add them to the bowl with the dressing. Mix well, then cover and leave to one side.

2 To make the sanjim, put the garlic, spring onions (scallions) and walnuts into a mini food processor, and blend into a coarse mix. Scoop into a serving bowl and add the soy sauce, chilli sauce, honey and sesame oil. Mix well, then cover and leave to one side.

3 To cook the steaks, heat a griddle over a high heat until smoking. Rub the olive oil over the steaks and season both sides with salt and pepper. Griddle the steaks for 2–3 minutes on each side until brilliantly charred and perfectly pink in the centre. Remove from the heat and leave to one side to rest.

4 Drain and rinse the carrots thoroughly under cold water. Repeat several times to remove all the salt. Squeeze out any excess water using your hands and add the carrots to the bowl with the dressing. Mix well and serve with the steaks and sanjim.

MOROCCAN CHICKEN, SPROUTING BROCCOLI & COUSCOUS

1 Heat a frying pan or skillet over a medium heat. Add the almonds and gently toast, shaking the pan occasionally, for 4–6 minutes, or until the almonds are a beautiful golden brown. Transfer the nuts to a plate to cool.

2 To make the spice paste, put all the ingredients in a mini food processor and blend to a smooth paste. Transfer to a large mixing bowl.

3 Add the chicken to the spice paste and mix well, making sure the chicken is completely coated. Cover and leave to marinate for 30 minutes, or overnight in the refrigerator if time allows.

4 Heat a griddle pan over a high heat and griddle the chicken for 5–6 minutes on each side, or until golden and cooked through. Set aside for a few minutes to rest and then slice into thin strips.

5 Tip the couscous into a large mixing bowl and pour over 250ml/9fl oz/1 cup warm water. Cover with cling film (plastic wrap) and leave for 10 minutes, or until tender, then fluff with a fork to separate the grains.

6 Meanwhile, bring a saucepan of water to the boil. Add the broccoli and cook for 3–4 minutes, or until just tender. Drain in a colander, then refresh in cold water and drain again.

7 Put the prepared chicken, broccoli, toasted almonds, mint, lemon juice and oil into the mixing bowl with the couscous and season with a good pinch of salt and pepper. Toss everything together until well combined and serve immediately.

SERVES 4
READY IN 1 HOUR

50g/1¾oz/⅓ cup almonds
500g/1lb 2oz boneless, skinless chicken thighs
150g/5½oz/heaped ¾ cup couscous
150g/5½oz sprouting broccoli, roughly chopped
2 large handfuls mint leaves, roughly chopped
juice of 1 lemon
2 tbsp olive oil
sea salt and freshly ground black pepper

For the spice paste
1 garlic clove
1 red chilli, deseeded
2.5cm/1in piece root ginger, peeled and roughly chopped
1 large handful mint leaves, roughly chopped
1 tsp ground cumin
½ tsp turmeric
juice of 1 lemon
2 tbsp olive oil
½ tsp sea salt

GRILLED CORIANDER & MINT CHICKEN

SERVES 4
READY IN 40 MINUTES

500g/1lb 2oz boneless, skinless
   chicken thighs
olive oil, for brushing

For the marinade
1 large handful mint leaves
1 large handful coriander
   (cilantro) leaves
1 green chilli, deseeded and
   roughly chopped
300ml/10½fl oz/scant 1¼ cups
   natural yogurt
2 tsp garam masala
juice of 1 lemon
sea salt

1 To make the marinade, put all the ingredients into a food processor and blend until smooth. Reserve half of the mixture to use as a sauce later and mix the rest with the chicken in a large mixing bowl until the chicken is completely coated. Cover and leave to marinate in the refrigerator for 30 minutes, or overnight if time allows.

2 Wipe the marinade off the chicken thighs to stop it from burning, then rub a little oil on both sides of all the pieces of chicken. Heat a griddle pan, or frying pan if you don't have one, until smoking, then cook the chicken for 5–6 minutes each side, or until golden and cooked through.

3 Slice the chicken into strips and serve immediately, topped with the reserved yogurt mixture.

RED SNAPPER WITH MEXICAN SALSA VERDE & CORN SALAD

SERVES 4
READY IN 20 MINUTES

2 tbsp olive oil, plus extra for
    brushing
4 red snapper fillets, skin on,
    about 120g/4¼oz each
250g/9oz cherry tomatoes,
    halved
165g/5¾oz/heaped ¾ cup
    sweetcorn
1 small handful mint leaves,
    finely chopped
juice of 1 lime
sea salt and freshly ground black
    pepper

For the mexican salsa verde
1 garlic clove, peeled
1 green jalapeño chilli
6 spring onions (scallions),
    trimmed
1 tomato
2 large handfuls coriander
    (cilantro) leaves
2 large handfuls mint leaves
2 large handfuls parsley leaves
juice of 3 limes
2 tbsp olive oil
sea salt and freshly ground black
    pepper

1 To make the salsa verde, put all the ingredients into a food processor with 100ml/3½ fl oz/⅓ cup water and blend until smooth.

2 Preheat the grill (broiler) to high. Brush a little oil over each piece of fish and season with salt and pepper. Place under the hot grill, skin side up, and grill for 2–3 minutes each side, or until just tender and flaky.

3 Meanwhile, in a mixing bowl, toss together the cherry tomatoes, sweetcorn, mint, lime juice and oil, and season with a good pinch of salt and pepper. Serve immediately with the grilled fish and vibrant salsa.

CHARRED PANEER WITH MINT CHUTNEY

SERVES 2
READY IN 10 MINUTES

1 green chilli
¼ red onion
2 large handfuls of mint leaves
½ tsp ground coriander
1 tomato
30g/1oz creamed coconut
½ lemon
150g/5½oz paneer
1 tbsp olive oil
sea salt

FOR MY VERSION OF THE CLASSIC INDIAN SNACK, GRILLED PANEER, I HAVE ADDED A LITTLE COCONUT TO THE CHUTNEY, AS IT WORKS SO WELL WITH THE MINT, CHILLI AND GROUND CORIANDER. IT ALSO SEEMS TO BRING ALL THOSE FRESH INGREDIENTS TOGETHER SO THAT THEIR FLAVOURS COMBINE INTO SOMETHING NEW. MR PANEER WALLAH ON UAH KHAM MURG IN SUNNY MUMBAI – I HOPE I HAVE DONE YOU PROUD.

1 Cut the top off the chilli and roll the chilli between your hands to deseed it, then put it into a mini food processor. Peel the onion and add it to the food processor. Strip in the mint leaves, then add the coriander, tomato, coconut and 3 tablespoons water, and season with salt. Squeeze in the juice from the lemon. Blend until smooth and pour into a serving bowl. Cover and leave to one side.

2 Heat a griddle over a high heat until smoking. Meanwhile, cut the paneer into pieces 1cm/½in thick and brush each piece with a little oil. Griddle for 1–1½ minutes on each side until charred with perfect griddle lines. Transfer to a serving plate and serve with the madly green mint chutney.

MEXICAN CHILLI–CHOCOLATE MOLE CHICKEN

1 First, make the mole. Heat a large frying pan or skillet over a medium heat, then add the garlic, peanuts and cloves to the pan. Toast for 4–5 minutes, shaking the pan occasionally, until the peanuts have started turning golden. While they toast, put the chillies in a bowl and pour over 2 tablespoons boiling water to soften them.

2 Put the toasted peanuts, cloves and garlic into a blender or food processor. Tip in the chillies and their soaking water and add the onion, tomatoes, cinnamon, cumin, oregano, brown sugar, three tablespoons of the oil and a really good pinch of salt. Blend for 2 minutes so that the sauce becomes beautifully smooth. Pour the sauce into a saucepan and bring to the boil over a medium heat. Cover, reduce the heat to low and simmer for 20 minutes.

3 Meanwhile, make the salad. Shave the fennel using a slicer or mandolin and add to a large mixing bowl with the radish. Pour in the lime juice and oil, and season with salt and pepper. Mix everything together really well, then cover and set aside.

4 To cook the chicken, heat a griddle until smoking and rub the remaining 2 tablespoons of olive oil all over the chicken breasts. Griddle for 10–12 minutes on each side until tender. Remove the pan from the heat and leave to one side.

5 When the mole sauce has simmered for 20 minutes, break in the chocolate and mix well. Cook for another 10 minutes, stirring occasionally, so that the flavours develop even more.

6 Make the polenta while the sauce finishes cooking. Pour the polenta into a saucepan and whisk in 800ml/28fl oz/scant 3½ cups boiling water. Cook over a low heat for 1–2 minutes, stirring continuously, until the water is absorbed and the polenta cooked. Stir in the butter and a good pinch of salt and pepper. Serve the polenta with the chicken, and pour the rich, velvety brown mole sauce over the top. Sprinkle each serving with sesame seeds and serve with the salad.

SERVES 4
READY IN 45 MINUTES

6 garlic cloves, peeled
55g/2oz/heaped ⅓ cup peanuts
4 cloves
2 chipotle chillies
1 onion, peeled and quartered
400g/14oz/scant 1⅔ cups tinned chopped tomatoes
1 tsp ground cinnamon
1½ tsp ground cumin
2 tsp dried oregano
2 tsp brown sugar
5 tbsp olive oil
4 skinless chicken breasts
30g/1oz dark chocolate (70–85% cocoa solids)
200g/7oz/1⅓ cups quick-cook polenta
25g/1oz butter

For the fennel salad
2 fennel bulbs
100g/3½oz radishes, quartered
juice of ½ lime
2 tbsp olive oil
sea salt and freshly ground black pepper

CUMIN, CHILLI & SOY RIBS

SERVES 4
READY IN 1 HOUR

8–12 pork belly ribs
olive oil, for brushing

For the sauce
3 tbsp vegetable oil
2 tsp cumin seeds
1 tsp chilli flakes
4 garlic cloves, finely chopped
6 spring onions (scallions), finely
 chopped
4 tbsp soy sauce
1 tbsp honey

1 Bring a large saucepan of water to the boil, then add the pork belly ribs. Turn the heat down and simmer for 45 minutes, or until the meat is tender and cooked through. Drain the ribs in a colander and allow to dry for a couple of minutes.

2 Meanwhile, make the sauce. Heat the oil in a small saucepan over a medium heat and chuck in the cumin seeds and chilli flakes. Allow them to crackle for 30 seconds until fragrant, then add 3 of the chopped garlic cloves and 5 of the chopped spring onions (scallions) and stir-fry for 2 minutes. Pour in the soy sauce, honey and 150ml/5fl oz/scant ⅔ cup hot water. Bring to the boil and cook, stirring occasionally, for about 4 minutes until the sauce has reduced and become sticky.

3 Preheat the grill (broiler) to high. Brush the ribs with the sauce and place them under the hot grill for 3–4 minutes on each side until golden brown. Be sure to brush with more sauce when you turn them over.

4 Place the grilled ribs on a large platter and serve with any leftover sauce on the side, or smother the ribs with the sauce. Sprinkle over the remaining chopped garlic and spring onion and serve immediately.

SWEET CHILLI & BASIL CHICKEN

I AM A SUCKER FOR CHICKEN WITH A DIP. THIS IS PROBABLY
A HANGOVER FROM MY DAD'S OBSESSION WITH CHICKEN
AND MAYONNAISE! MY CHEEKY CHICKEN SNACK USES LITTLE
CHICKEN FILLETS THAT COOK IN NO TIME. IT'S SERVED WITH
A PUNCHY DIPPING SAUCE THAT IS MADE WITH SWEET CHILLI
SAUCE, FRESH GREEN BASIL AND WONDERFUL FENNEL SEEDS,
WHICH LIVEN IT UP WITH A BACKGROUND HINT OF ANISEED.

1 Heat a griddle over a high heat until smoking. Meanwhile,
brush the chicken with ½ tablespoon of the oil. Lay it in
the griddle and reduce the heat to medium. Griddle the
chicken for 3–4 minutes on each side until golden and
cooked through.

2 While the chicken cooks, put the basil, the remaining
oil and a good pinch of salt and pepper into a mini food
processor or blender, and blend until smooth. Pour the oil
mixture into a serving bowl. Gently crush the fennel seeds
with the back of a knife or using a mortar and pestle, and
add them to the serving bowl. Add the sweet chilli sauce
nd lime juice, and mix well. Serve the golden chicken with
the sweet chilli and basil sauce.

SERVES 2
READY IN 10 MINUTES

4 mini chicken fillets (about
    200g/7oz total weight)
2½ tbsp olive oil
1 handful of basil leaves
1 tsp fennel seeds
3 tbsp sweet chilli sauce
juice of ½ lime
sea salt and freshly ground
    black pepper

STEWS

STICKY SZECHUAN PORK

SERVES 4
READY IN 1 HOUR 45 MINUTES

2 tbsp vegetable oil

4 dried red chillies, roughly chopped

6 star anise

500g/1lb 2oz boneless pork belly, cut into 2.5cm/1in-wide pieces

2.5cm/1in piece root ginger, roughly sliced

1 tsp sea salt

1 tbsp rice vinegar

2 tbsp sugar

1 tbsp soy sauce

1 tbsp sesame seeds

THIS RECIPE IS CHINESE COOKING AT IT'S BEST – THE PORK BELLY IS COOKED SLOWLY WITH THE SPICES, SO IT FULLY ABSORBS ALL THEIR DELICIOUS SZECHUAN FLAVOURS, AND IS THEN COATED IN A RICH STICKY SAUCE. YOU CAN LEAVE THE SKIN OF THE ROOT GINGER ON WHEN PREPARING THIS DISH. NOT ONLY DOES THIS MAKE THE PREPARATION QUICKER, BUT ACCORDING TO A FRIEND OF MINE, MR HUNG, IN CHENGDU, THE SKIN ADDS A BETTER FLAVOUR AND IS VERY HEALTHY TO EAT. FRANKLY, LESS PEELING CAN ONLY BE A GOOD THING! JUST MAKE SURE THE GINGER IS FRESH AND THAT YOU GIVE IT A GOOD WASH BEFORE YOU SLICE IT.

1 Heat the oil in a wok over a high heat. When smoking hot, chuck in the dried red chillies and star anise and stir-fry for 30 seconds until fragrant. Add the pork belly, ginger and salt, and continue to stir-fry for 2–3 minutes, or until the pork starts to take on a little colour.

2 Pour over 500ml/17fl oz/2 cups hot water, which should just cover everything, and give it a good stir. Bring to the boil, cover, reduce the heat to low and simmer for 1 hour 30 minutes, or until the pork is cooked through and tender. Remove the pork from the wok with a slotted spoon and set aside. Skim off any excess fat from the surface of the liquid left in the wok using a spoon.

3 Whisk together the vinegar, sugar, soy sauce and 1 tablespoon water in a small bowl and then add to the wok. Turn the heat up to high and cook, stirring continuously, for 5 minutes, or until the sauce has reduced by half.

4 Return the pork to the wok, add the sesame seeds, then stir-fry for 2–3 minutes, or until the sauce has become really thick and sticky and the pork is well coated. Sprinkle over the sesame seeds and serve immediately.

PERSIAN SAFFRON & HONEY LAMB

THE EARTHY SMELL OF SAFFRON EVOKES THE WINDY
SOUKS, SWEET MINT TEAS, COLOURFUL SPICE MARKETS
AND BEAUTIFUL MOSQUES THAT INSPIRED ME TO MAKE THIS
WONDERFUL PERSIAN STEW. THE SAFFRON AND CINNAMON
ARE ALL YOU NEED TO PROVIDE A REAL DEPTH OF FLAVOUR
AND THE HONEY AND APRICOTS LEND JUST THE RIGHT AMOUNT
OF SWEETNESS, WHICH WORKS PERFECTLY WITH THE LAMB.
THIS STEW IS RICH BUT LIGHT AND FULL OF FLAVOUR FROM
SUCH AMAZING SPICES.

SERVES 4
READY IN 2 HOURS

500g/1lb 2oz lamb leg, cut into
    2.5cm/1in cubes
2 tbsp olive oil
1 large onion, finely chopped
400g/14oz tinned chickpeas,
    washed and drained
a small pinch of saffron, about
    4–6 strands
5cm/2in cinnamon stick
1 tbsp honey
100g/3½oz/⅔ cup dried apricots
sea salt and freshly ground black
    pepper
juice of ½ lemon, to serve
1 handful parsley leaves,
    chopped, to serve
steamed rice, to serve

1 Season the meat with a really good pinch of salt and pepper.
Heat the oil in a large flameproof casserole dish (Dutch oven)
over a medium heat, then add the lamb in batches and cook,
turning occasionally, for 10 minutes until browned all over.
Remove with a slotted spoon and set aside.

2 Add the onion to the pan and stir-fry for 3–4 minutes,
or until it starts to turn golden. Return the lamb to the
pan and add the chickpeas, saffron, cinnamon and 600ml/
21fl oz/scant 2½ cups freshly boiled water, which should be
enough to just cover everything. Season with a good pinch
of salt and pepper and gently mix together. Bring to the boil,
cover, reduce the heat to low and simmer gently for 1 hour,
or until the meat is cooked through and tender.

3 Add the honey and apricots, increase the heat to medium
and cook, uncovered, stirring occasionally, for 20 minutes,
or until the sauce has reduced a little.

4 Remove from the heat, cover and set aside for 5–10 minutes
for the stew to rest a little before it is served. Pour over the
lemon juice, then scatter over the chopped parsley and serve
immediately with steamed rice.

BERBER BEEF STEW

SERVES 4
READY IN 45 MINUTES

2 tbsp olive oil
1 carrot, peeled and chopped
    into 1cm/½in half-moons
2 courgettes (zucchini),
    chopped into 1cm/½in
    half-moons
600g/1lb 5oz beef fillet, cut
    into 2–3cm/¾–½in cubes
1 red onion, peeled and finely
    chopped
4 garlic cloves, peeled and finely
    chopped
2 tbsp tomato purée (paste)
2 tsp ground cumin
2 tsp ground ginger
1 tsp paprika
1 tsp freshly ground black
    pepper
½ tsp ground cinnamon
1 tsp flour
1 tbsp clear honey
150g/5½oz/heaped ¾ cup
    couscous
1 preserved lemon
200g/7oz/heaped ¾ cup yogurt
2 tbsp harissa paste
1 large handful of parsley leaves,
    finely chopped
2 tbsp toasted flaked almonds
sea salt

1 Heat the oil in a large saucepan over a high heat and add the carrots and courgettes (zucchini). Cook for 4 minutes, stirring frequently, to soften.

2 Add the beef, onion and garlic to the cooked vegetables and mix well. Reduce the heat to medium, add the tomato purée (paste), cumin, ground ginger, paprika, black pepper, cinnamon, flour, honey and 250ml/9fl oz/1 cup boiling water. Mix well, bring to the boil, then cover and simmer for 10 minutes, or until the beef is just cooked through.

3 While the beef cooks, put the couscous in a large mixing bowl and add 185ml/6fl oz/¾ cup warm water. Cover with cling film (plastic wrap) and leave for 10 minutes or until ready to eat.

4 Remove the flesh from the preserved lemon and finely chop the skin. Leave to one side. Discard the flesh. Tip the yogurt into a serving bowl, then stir in the harissa, cover and leave to one side.

5 Remove the lid from the cooked stew, turn the heat up to medium and cook for another 5 minutes, stirring occasionally, so that the sauce becomes lovely and thick. Throw the parsley and preserved lemon skin into the cooked stew, and mix well. Fluff up the couscous with a fork and divide into four bowls. Spoon over the stew, top with the almonds and serve with the harissa yogurt.

MOROCCAN CINNAMON & LEMON CHICKEN

SERVES 4
READY IN 1 HOUR 30 MINUTES

2 tbsp olive oil

1 onion, roughly sliced

2.5cm/1in cinnamon stick

2 large tomatoes, roughly chopped

½ tsp turmeric

¼ tsp freshly ground black pepper

1.5kg/3lb 5oz chicken legs and thighs on the bone, skinned

300g/10½oz small waxy potatoes, roughly sliced

1 unwaxed lemon, thinly sliced and pips removed

2 large handfuls parsley leaves, finely chopped

sea salt

1 Preheat the oven to 190°C/375°F/Gas 5. Heat the oil in an flameproof casserole dish over a medium heat, then add the onion and cinnamon. Cook, stirring occasionally, for 6–7 minutes, or until the onion is just turning golden.

2 Add the tomatoes, turmeric, black pepper and season with a good pinch of salt. Mix everything together well and then add the chicken. Cover the chicken with alternate layers of potato and lemon slices (the order doesn't matter), then pour over enough freshly boiled water to just cover everything. Put the casserole dish in the preheated oven with the lid on, then cook for 1 hour, or until the chicken is cooked through and beautifully tender.

3 Return the casserole dish to the hob over a medium heat, remove the lid and cook for 15 minutes, stirring occasionally and very gently, so the sauce can reduce. Gently stir in the chopped parsley and serve immediately.

MEXICAN ORANGE & ALMOND CHICKEN

1 Heat the oil in a flameproof casserole dish (Dutch oven) over a high heat. Add the chicken thighs and cook, skin-side down, for 3–4 minutes, or until the skin has turned a lovely golden colour. Turn the chicken thighs over, chuck in the garlic and cook for a further 30 seconds until fragrant. Pour in the stock and bring to the boil. Cover, reduce the heat to low and simmer gently for 20 minutes, or until the chicken is just cooked through and tender.

2 Meanwhile, heat a medium frying pan or skillet over a medium-high heat, then add the jalapeño chillies and red (bell) peppers. Char them, turning occasionally, for 3–4 minutes or until they develop a few really blackened areas. This will provide the lovely smoky flavour so typical of Mexican cooking. Once cool enough to touch, skin and deseed the chillies and remove any really charred bits from the peppers. Finely slice the pieces of pepper and the chillies.

3 Put the almonds into a food processor and pulse a few times. You want the almonds to be fairly well ground, but still retain some chunky texture.

4 Bring the chicken back to the boil over a medium heat, then add the chillies, peppers, almonds, spring onions (scallions) and orange juice and season with a really good pinch of salt and pepper. Mix everything together so it is well combined and cook for 10 minutes.

5 Add the yogurt, reduce the heat to low and simmer gently, stirring occasionally, for a further 10 minutes, or until the sauce is like a lovely thick soup. Serve immediately with tortilla chips on the side.

SERVES 4
READY IN 50 MINUTES

2 tbsp olive oil
4 chicken thighs on the bone, about 150–200g/5½–7oz each
2 garlic cloves, finely chopped
300ml/10½fl oz/scant 1¼ cups chicken stock
2 red jalapeño chillies
2 red (bell) peppers, deseeded and cut into 8 pieces each
50g/1¾oz/⅓ cup blanched almonds
4 spring onions (scallions), finely chopped
juice of 1 orange
270ml/9½fl oz/1 cup thick Greek-style yogurt
sea salt and freshly ground black pepper
tortilla chips, to serve

PUEBLAN ALMOND DUCK

SERVES 4
READY IN 45 MINUTES

4 duck breasts, skin on, about
   175–200g/6–7oz each
5 tbsp olive oil
4 tomatoes, roughly chopped
30g/1oz French bread, roughly
   torn into bite-sized pieces
60g/2¼oz/heaped ⅓ cup
   almonds
5cm/2in cinnamon stick
6 whole cloves
2 dried red chillies
300ml/10½fl oz/scant 1¼ cups
   chicken stock
sea salt and freshly ground black
   pepper
1 tbsp flaked almonds, toasted,
   to serve

1 Remove the duck breasts from the refrigerator at least
30 minutes before cooking, so they are not too cold to cook
perfectly in the middle.

2 Heat 3 tablespoons of the oil in a large saucepan over
a medium heat, then add the tomatoes, French bread,
almonds, cinnamon, cloves and dried red chillies. Give
everything a good stir, so it all gets coated in the oil. Fry
for 4–5 minutes, or until the tomatoes start to break down,
stirring occasionally so nothing burns. Pour the tomato
mixture into a food processor with 200ml/7fl oz/scant
1 cup water, then blend for 4–5 minutes until smooth.

3 Pour back into the pan and add the stock, stir well and bring
to the boil over a high heat. Reduce the heat to low and
simmer gently, partially covered, for 25 minutes. This will
allow the liquid to reduce slightly and the flavours to develop.

4 Meanwhile, season the duck breasts on both sides with a little
salt and pepper. Heat the remaining 2 tablespoons of oil in
a large frying pan or skillet over a medium heat, then cook
the duck breasts for 5–6 minutes on each side, or until they
are golden on the outside but still pink in the middle. Remove
the duck breasts from the pan, slice into 3 or 4 pieces and
then return to the pan.

5 Reheat the sauce, then pour over the duck breasts.
Leave to rest for 5 minutes, then serve scattered with
the flaked almonds.

ESSAOUIRA MONKFISH TAGINE

1 Cut the monkfish into 2 pieces and put them in a mixing bowl. Pour over the juice from the lemon and add a pinch of salt. Mix together and leave to one side. Tip the couscous into a large mixing bowl and add 185ml/6fl oz/¾ cup warm water. Cover with cling film (plastic wrap) and leave for a minimum of 10 minutes, or until ready to eat.

2 Heat the oil in a large saucepan over a high heat and add the peppers and carrots. Cook for 5–6 minutes, stirring occasionally, until they start to soften. Reduce the heat to medium and add the garlic, cumin, paprika, black pepper, chilli powder, sugar and a pinch of salt, and mix well.

3 Tip in the tomatoes, pour over 200ml/7fl oz/scant 1 cup hot water and mix everything together really well. Bring to the boil and add the fish. Cover, leaving a small gap, and cook for 5–6 minutes. Turn the fish over, spoon some sauce over the top, then re-cover and cook for another 5–6 minutes until the fish is cooked through and tender.

4 While the fish cooks, remove the flesh from the preserved lemon and slice the skin into thin strips. Discard the flesh. Fluff up the couscous with a fork. Chuck the preserved lemon skin, olives and parsley into the pan with the cooked fish, and mix well. To serve, cut the pieces of fish in half and serve with the couscous.

SERVES 4
READY IN 30 MINUTES

600g/1lb 5oz monkfish fillet, membrane removed
juice of ½ lemon
150g/5½oz/heaped ¾ cup couscous
3 tbsp olive oil
2 red (bell) peppers, deseeded and finely sliced
2 carrots, peeled and sliced into rounds
4 garlic cloves, peeled
2 tsp ground cumin
1 tsp paprika
½ tsp freshly ground black pepper
¼ tsp chilli powder
1 tsp sugar
400g/14oz/scant 1⅔ cups tinned chopped tomatoes
1 preserved lemon
30g/1oz/¼ cup pitted black olives, sliced
1 large handful of parsley leaves, finely chopped
sea salt

CONDESA SMOKY BEANS

1 Cook the rice in boiling water for 10–12 minutes until soft, or as directed on the packet. Drain in a colander, then cover the rice with a clean tea towel while still in the colander and leave to one side. Meanwhile, put the chipotle chilli in a small bowl, cover with 2–3 tablespoons boiling water and leave to one side to soften for a couple of minutes.

2 Heat the oil in a large saucepan over a high heat and add the pepper and onion. Stir-fry for 3 minutes to soften, then reduce the heat to medium and add the bay leaves and garlic, and mix well.

3 Add the cinnamon, cumin, tomatoes, honey and beans to the onion mixture. Season with salt. Pour in the chipotle and its water. Mix well, then cover and cook for 15 minutes, stirring occasionally, or until the beans are hot and the sauce is thick.

4 Make the green salsa. Cut the avocado in half and remove the stone with a knife. Scoop out the flesh into a blender or food processor. Discard the top of the chilli, then chuck it into the blender with the spring onions (scallions), coriander (cilantro), oil and some salt. Add the lime juice and blend into a coarse salsa. Tip into a serving bowl. Serve the rice and beans with the cheese grated over the top and with the salsa.

SERVES 4
READY IN 30 MINUTES

250g/9oz/1¼ cups long grain rice
1 chipotle chilli, halved
800g/1lb.12oz/4 cups tinned pinto beans, drained and rinsed
2 tbsp olive oil
1 red (bell) pepper, deseeded and finely chopped
1 red onion, peeled and finely chopped
2 bay leaves
4 garlic cloves, peeled and crushed
1 tsp ground cinnamon
2 tsp ground cumin
400g/14oz/scant 1⅔ cups tinned chopped tomatoes
1½ tbsp clear honey
55g/2oz Gruyère cheese
sea salt

For the green salsa
1 avocado
3 spring onions (scallions), trimmed
1 green chilli
2 large handfuls of coriander (cilantro) leaves and stalks
2 tbsp olive oil
juice of 1 lime

MEATY
MAINS

SHREDDED BEEF TACOS

1 Bring a large saucepan of water to the boil. Add the beef, turn the heat down to low and simmer gently for 30 minutes until the beef is cooked through. Remove the beef from the water and set aside to cool.

2 Meanwhile, heat the oil in a large saucepan over a medium heat. Add the onion and garlic and cook, stirring occasionally, for 6–8 minutes, or until the onion is lovely and golden. Add the tomatoes, oregano, thyme, green jalapeño chilli, vinegar, tomato purée (paste) and sugar and season with a really good pinch of salt and pepper. Reduce the heat to low, cover and cook for 20 minutes, then remove the lid and cook, stirring occasionally, for a further 10 minutes, or until the mixture gets really thick.

3 Flake the cooked beef into small pieces and add to the pan with the tomato sauce. Mix well, turn the heat up to medium and cook for 3–4 minutes, or until the beef is hot all the way through.

4 To assemble the tacos, place a good tablespoonful of beef into the centre of each tortilla with a generous dollop of soured cream. Scatter over some lettuce, radish and feta. Roll up or leave open, as liked, and serve immediately.

SERVES 4
READY IN 1 HOUR
15 MINUTES

500g/1lb 2oz braising or flank steak
2 tbsp olive oil
1 small onion, finely chopped
3 garlic cloves, finely chopped
4 tomatoes, finely chopped
½ tsp dried oregano
½ tsp dried thyme
1 green jalapeño chilli, deseeded and finely chopped
1 tbsp white wine vinegar or cider vinegar
1 tbsp tomato purée (paste)
a pinch of sugar
8 small flour tortillas, grilled (broiled) (optional)
200ml/7fl oz/scant 1 cup soured cream
1 small cos lettuce, finely sliced
4 radishes, finely sliced
75g/2½oz feta cheese
sea salt and freshly ground black pepper

FIVE-SPICE PORK BELLY

MUSTARD IS A CLASSIC ACCOMPANIMENT TO CRISPY PORK BELLY IN HONG KONG – IT WORKS WELL AND CUTS THROUGH THE RICHNESS OF THE MEAT. GET YOUR BUTCHER OR SUPERMARKET MEAT-COUNTER ASSISTANT TO SCORE THE FAT OF THE PORK BELLY TO HELP SAVE YOU LOADS OF PREPARATION TIME.

SERVES 4
READY IN 40 MINUTES

1.25kg/2lb 12oz piece pork belly, skin scored
4 tsp Chinese five-spice powder
1 tsp ground Sichuan pepper
sea salt
250g/9oz/1¼ cups jasmine rice
200g/7oz pak choi (bok choy), cut into quarters
85g/3oz/scant ⅓ cup French mustard

For the dipping sauce
3 tbsp soy sauce
1 tbsp rice wine vinegar
2 tbsp clear honey
¼ tsp chilli powder
1 garlic clove, peeled and crushed

1 Preheat the oven to 250°C/500°F/Gas 9. Cut the pork belly into 2 pieces to help it cook quicker, and put both pieces, skin-side up, in a roasting tin. Rub the skin with the Chinese five-spice powder, ground Sichuan pepper and a good pinch of salt. Put it into the oven, reduce the heat to 220°C/425°F/Gas 7 and cook for 30–35 minutes until the pork is cooked through and the skin is madly crispy.

2 Meanwhile, make the dipping sauce. Pour the soy sauce into a serving bowl and add 2 tablespoons water, the rice wine vinegar and honey. Add the chilli powder and garlic, and whisk together, then cover and leave to one side to allow the flavours to develop.

3 Cook the rice in boiling water for 10–12 minutes until soft, or as directed on the packet, then drain in a colander. Pour boiling water into the saucepan to a depth of 2.5cm/1in and heat over a low heat. Put the colander with the rice over the pan and leave to steam gently until you are ready to eat.

4 When the pork has cooked for 25 minutes, put the pak choi (bok choy) into a steamer and steam over a high heat for 5 minutes, or until just tender. Divide the sticky rice into four serving bowls and tip the mustard into a serving dish. Carve the pork and serve with the rice, pak choi, dipping sauce and mustard.

THAI PORK WITH LEMONGRASS & LIME DIPPING SAUCE

SERVES 4
READY IN 40 MINUTES

600g/1lb 5oz pork tenderloin, trimmed and cut into 10cm/4in pieces
4 garlic cloves, crushed
1 tsp freshly ground black pepper
½ tsp sugar
1 tbsp rice wine
2 tbsp fish sauce
3 tbsp groundnut (peanut) oil
150g/5½oz green beans, halved
200g/7oz medium egg noodles
juice of ½ lime

For the lemongrass and lime dipping sauce
2 lemongrass stalks, trimmed and tough outer leaves removed
1cm/½in piece fresh root ginger, peeled
1 handful of coriander (cilantro) leaves and stalks
½ tsp chilli powder
2 tsp sugar
1 tbsp fish sauce
juice of 1½ limes

1 Preheat the oven to 200°C/400°F/Gas 6. Put the pieces of pork into an ovenproof dish, then peel add the garlic, black pepper, sugar, rice wine, 1 tablespoon of the fish sauce and 1 tablespoon of the oil. Mix everything together well and roast for 30–35 minutes until the pork is just cooked through and tender.

2 Meanwhile, to make the dipping sauce, put the lemongrass and ginger into a mini food processorand add the coriander (cilantro) leaves and stalks, chilli powder, sugar, fish sauce, lime juice and 4 tablespoons water. Blend into a smooth sauce and pour into a serving bowl. Cover and leave to one side so that all the amazing savoury flavours come together.

3 Cook the beans and noodles in boiling water for 4–5 minutes until the noodles are soft, or as directed on the packet. Drain and return to the saucepan. Pour in the remaining 2 tablespoons of oil and 1 tablespoon of fish sauce, then add the lime juice. Mix well, cover and leave to one side until the pork is ready. Slice the pork and serve with the noodles and the dipping sauce alongside.

LAO LAP AUBERGINES & PORK

1 Heat 3 tablespoons of the oil in a large frying pan or skillet over a medium-low heat and add half of the sliced garlic and half of the chilli. Mix well and cook, stirring occasionally, while you prepare the aubergines (eggplants).

2 Slice the aubergines into 5mm/¼in discs and layer them in the pan. Pour over 1 tablespoon of the fish sauce and 2 tablespoons water. Cover and cook for 20 minutes, or until tender, shaking the pan occasionally and turning the aubergines halfway through cooking. Remove the lid and pour in 2 tablespoons of the soy sauce. Turn the heat up to medium and cook for 4–5 minutes, shaking the pan occasionally, until the aubergines have taken on a little colour.

3 Meanwhile, cook the rice in boiling water for 10–12 minutes until soft, or as directed on the packet, then drain in a colander. Put the lemongrass, remaining chilli and remaining garlic into a mini food processor. Blend into a rough paste. Finely chop half the herbs and leave to one side.

4 Heat a wok over a high heat until smoking. Add the remaining oil and the pork. Stir-fry for 2 minutes, then add the spice paste and stir-fry for another 2–3 minutes until the pork is just cooked through. Add the remaining fish sauce and soy sauce along with the lime juice and stir-fry for 1 minute. Turn off the heat, chuck in the chopped herbs, mix well and leave to one side. Put the cooked aubergines on a large serving plate, spoon over the pork and top with the remaining herbs and the bean sprouts. Serve with the rice.

SERVES 4
READY IN 30 MINUTES

5 tbsp groundnut (peanut) oil
6 garlic cloves, peeled and sliced
2 red chillies, sliced
2 aubergines (eggplants)
2 tbsp fish sauce
3 tbsp dark soy sauce
250g/9oz/1¼ cups jasmine rice
2 lemongrass stalks, trimmed
    and tough outer leaves
    removed
1 handful of dill
1 handful of coriander (cilantro)
    leaves
1 handful of mint leaves
500g/1lb 2oz minced (ground)
    pork
juice of 1 lime
1 handful of bean sprouts

CHORIZO *&* CHILLI FOCACCIA

THIS SUPER-FAST DISH IS BASICALLY AN OPEN SANDWICH.
THE CHORIZO FILLING DOES MOST OF THE WORK AND THE
FENNEL SEEDS, CHILLI AND GARLIC MAKE IT TASTE EVEN
BETTER. JUICY CHERRY TOMATOES, PEPPERY ROCKET AND
SALTY PECORINO ADD ALL THE EXTRA FLAVOURS YOU NEED
TO MAKE ONE HECK OF A SANDWICH – AND IT ONLY TAKES
10 MINUTES TO PREPARE AND COOK.

SERVES 2
READY IN 10 MINUTES

200g/7oz focaccia

1½ tbsp olive oil, plus extra to
serve

150g/5½oz chorizo, in one piece

2 garlic cloves, peeled and sliced

1 tsp fennel seeds

¼ tsp crushed chilli flakes

100g/3½oz/heaped ⅔ cup
cherry tomatoes, cut into
quarters

1 lemon

2 handfuls of rocket (arugula)

30g/1oz pecorino cheese

1 Preheat the grill (broiler) to high. Meanwhile, cut the
focaccia in half horizontally and carefully scoop out a little
of the centre from each half using your fingers. Drizzle
½ tablespoon of the oil over both halves and grill for
2½–3 minutes until golden.

2 While the focaccia cooks, slice the chorizo into bite-sized
pieces. Heat the remaining oil in a frying pan or skillet
over a medium heat and add the chorizo, garlic, fennel
seeds and chilli flakes. Mix everything together well and
cook for 3–4 minutes, stirring occasionally, until the chorizo
starts turning golden at the edges.

3 Place the grilled (broiled) foccacia on a chopping board
and put the cherry tomatoes into the centre of each.
Cut the lemon in half and squeeze the juice from 1 half into
the pan with the chorizo, then mix well. Tip the delicious
golden chorizo on to the focaccia, along with all the juices
from the pan. Scatter over the rocket (arugula) and shave
over the cheese. Serve with the remaining lemon and a bottle
of olive oil at the table.

MANCHURIAN LAMB WITH TAMARIND SLAW & GRIDDLED CHILLI POTATOES

1 Preheat the oven to 200°C/400°F/Gas 6. Put half the Sichuan pepper, sesame seeds and cumin seeds into a spice grinder and grind until smooth. Tip into a serving bowl and add the remaining spices and a good pinch of salt. Mix together really well.

2 If using loin fillet, pull off the membrane. Cut the lamb into 7.5–10cm/3–4in pieces and put in a small roasting tin. Pour over the olive oil and mix well. Sprinkle over two-thirds of the mixed spices and rub all over the lamb. Roast for 15–20 minutes until cooked through and really tender.

3 Meanwhile, boil the potatoes for 12–15 minutes until tender. While the lamb and potatoes cook, make the slaw. Mix the tamarind paste, honey, soy sauce, sesame oil and 2 tablespoons water in a mixing bowl. Grate the cabbage using the fine setting of a food processor, then tip into the bowl with the dressing. Chuck the spring onions (scallions), chilli and coriander (cilantro) into the bowl with the cabbage and toss together. Tip into a serving bowl, then cover.

4 Heat a griddle over a high heat. Meanwhile, drain the cooked potatoes and return them to the pan. Pour in the chilli oil and add a pinch of the mixed spices and a small pinch of salt. Mix well, and don't be afraid to break up a few of the potatoes. Tip the potatoes on to the hot griddle and cook for 2 minutes on each side, or until they start to crisp up, shaking the pan occasionally. Slice the lamb and sprinkle a little of the spices over the top. Serve with the potatoes and slaw, with the remaining spices at the table.

SERVES 4
READY IN 40 MINUTES

1 tsp Sichuan pepper
2 tbsp sesame seeds
2 tsp cumin seeds
600g/1lb 5oz trimmed neck or
    loin lamb fillet
2 tbsp olive oil
sea salt

For the griddled potatoes
500g/1lb 2oz new potatoes
2 tbsp chilli oil

For the tamarind slaw
2 tbsp tamarind paste
3 tsp clear honey
2 tsp soy sauce
2 tsp sesame oil
450g/1lb white cabbage
4 spring onions (scallions),
    trimmed and finely sliced
½ red chilli, finely chopped
1 handful of coriander (cilantro)
    leaves, finely chopped

STICKY MALAYSIAN LAMB WITH PENANG GARDEN RICE

SERVES 4
READY IN 40 MINUTES

4 lamb rump steaks (about 150g/5½oz each)
1 tsp Chinese five-spice powder
2 tbsp rice wine
2 tbsp oyster sauce
1 tbsp light soy sauce
1 tsp sesame oil
1 tsp olive oil

For the Penang rice
350g/12oz/1¾ cups basmati rice
2 lemongrass stalks
2 tbsp groundnut (peanut) oil
1 tsp fenugreek seeds
2.5cm/1in cinnamon stick
4 cardamom pods
3 star anise
2.5cm/1in piece fresh root ginger, peeled and finely chopped
1 onion, peeled and finely chopped
400ml/14fl oz/generous 1½ cups coconut milk
3 tbsp fish sauce
1 small handful of coriander (cilantro) leaves, roughly chopped

1 Preheat the oven to 200°C/400°F/Gas 6. Put the lamb in a small roasting tin and add the Chinese five-spice powder, rice wine, oyster sauce, soy sauce, sesame oil and olive oil. Mix well and leave to one side to marinate.

2 Put the rice in a large saucepan, cover with cold water and stir, and then leave to one side for 5 minutes to soak.

3 Bash the fat ends of the lemongrass with a wooden spoon. Heat the groundnut (peanut) oil in a shallow saucepan over a medium heat and add the fenugreek, cinnamon, cardamom and star anise. Stir-fry for 30 seconds until fragrant, then add the onion and ginger. Cook for 4–5 minutes, stirring occasionally, until the onion has started to turn golden.

4 Meanwhile, pop the lamb into the oven for 15–20 minutes until cooked through and tender.

5 Tip the soaked rice into a colander, then add it to the pan with the cooked onion and spices. Pour over 400ml/14fl oz/generous 1½ cups hot water and the coconut milk. Pop the lemongrass in the pan, then stir and cover. Reduce the heat to low and simmer gently for 10–15 minutes until all the water has been absorbed and the rice is tender. You can always add extra hot water if the rice needs it. Slice the cooked lamb.

6 Season the cooked rice with the fish sauce, then tip into a serving dish. Serve the lamb on the rice, sprinkled with coriander (cilantro).

LEBANESE LAMB WITH AUBERGINE RICE

1 Brush a little oil on both sides of the aubergine (eggplant) slices. Heat a griddle pan over a high heat, and when smoking, add the aubergines. Griddle for 2–3 minutes on each side until tender and covered in charred griddle lines. Set aside.

2 Heat a frying pan or skillet over a medium heat. Add the pine nuts and gently toast, shaking the pan occasionally, for 2–3 minutes, or until the pine nuts are golden brown. Transfer the nuts to a plate and set aside.

3 Heat 2 tablespoons of the oil in a large frying pan or skillet over a medium heat, then add the lamb, onion and garlic. Fry for 10–12 minutes, or until the lamb has started to turn golden, stirring occassionally. Add the tomatoes, cinnamon and allspice, season with salt and pepper, and cook for 5–6 minutes, or until the tomatoes have started to break down.

4 Put the rice into a large bowl, cover with cold water and stir, and then set aside for 5 minutes to soak. Tip the rice into a colander and give it a really good rinse under the cold tap, until the water runs clear. This washes the starch out of the rice and ensures you get lovely separated grains.

5 Tip the washed rice into the frying pan and place over a medium heat. Add the spiced lamb and stir in 600ml/21fl oz/ scant 2½ cups boiled water. Bring to the boil, cover, reduce the heat to low and simmer gently for 10–15 minutes, or until all the water has been absorbed and the rice is almost cooked but still has a little bite. Scatter over half the pine nuts and mix everything together with a fork.

6 Preheat the oven to 180°C/350°F/Gas 4. Drizzle the bottom of an ovenproof dish with a little oil. Arrange half the charred aubergines across the bottom of the dish, spread all of the rice and lamb mixture on top and then lay the other half of the aubergines on top of the rice. Scatter over the remaining toasted pine nuts and drizzle over a little more oil. Cover with tin foil and bake for 10 minutes. Serve immediately.

SERVES 4
READY IN 1 HOUR

4 tbsp olive oil, plus extra for brushing
1 large aubergine (eggplant), sliced lengthways into 5mm/¼in-thick strips
100g/3½oz/ ⅔ cup pine nuts
300g/10½oz minced (ground) lamb
1 onion, finely chopped
2 garlic cloves, finely chopped
2 large tomatoes, finely chopped
5cm/2in cinnamon stick
¼ tsp ground allspice
350g/12oz/1¾ cups basmati rice
sea salt and freshly ground black pepper

ROASTED LAMB LEG
WITH SPICED LENTIL PURÉE

1 Put the cumin, coriander, cinnamon, nutmeg and oil in a large mixing bowl, then add a good pinch of salt and mix well. Add the lamb to the bowl and rub in the paste until the lamb is well coated. Cover with cling film (plastic wrap) and set aside for at least 2 hours, or overnight in the refrigerator if time allows.

2 Preheat the oven to 200°C/400°F/Gas 6, leaving a roasting rack over a tray in the oven to heat up. Carefully place the seasoned lamb onto the roasting rack, skin side up, and roast for 30–35 minutes, or until the lamb is beautifully browned and crispy on the outside and juicy and pink in the middle. Remove from the oven, squeeze over the lemon juice and season with a good pinch of salt. Cover with foil and leave to rest for 10 minutes so the meat will be even more tender and delicious.

3 Meanwhile, cook the lentils in a large pan of boiling water for 12–15 minutes, or until they are cooked through and soft. Drain and set aside.

4 Heat the oil in a large saucepan over a medium heat, then add the onion and garlic and gently fry, stirring occasionally, for 6–8 minutes, or until golden. Throw in the cumin and coriander, and cook for 30 seconds, stirring frequently, until fragrant. Add the cooked lentils, lemon juice and 240ml/8fl oz/scant 1 cup freshly boiled water and season with a really good pinch of salt and pepper. Use a hand blender to purée the lentils until they are lovely and smooth, adding a little more water if the mixture gets too thick. Scatter in the parsley and gently mix to combine.

5 Finely slice the lamb and divide between the serving plates. Spoon over any juices from the grilling tray, add a good dollop of the lentil purée to the top of the lamb and a drizzle of oil, then serve immediately.

SERVES 4–6
READY IN 50 MINUTES,
   PLUS RESTING

1 tbsp ground cumin
2 tsp ground coriander
½ tsp ground cinnamon
a pinch of grated nutmeg
4 tbsp olive oil, plus extra for
   drizzling
1 lamb leg, about 1.6kg/3lb 8oz,
   butterflied
juice of ½ lemon
sea salt

For the lentil purée
200g/7oz/heaped 1 cup green
   lentils, washed and drained
2 tbsp olive oil
1 onion, finely chopped
2 garlic cloves, finely chopped
1 tsp ground cumin
1 tsp ground coriander
juice of 1 lemon
1 handful parsley leaves, finely
   chopped
sea salt and freshly ground black
   pepper

BEAUTIFUL BEEF MEZZE

SERVES 4
READY IN 40 MINUTES

600g/1lb 5oz beef fillet
4 garlic cloves, peeled
2 tsp paprika
2 tsp ground cumin
1 tsp ground coriander
2 tbsp olive oil
1 lemon
sea salt and freshly ground black
    pepper
4 flatbreads, to serve

For the spinach raita
30g/1oz/scant ¼ cup pine nuts
2 garlic cloves, peeled and sliced
2 tbsp olive oil
200g/7oz baby spinach
225g/8oz/scant 1 cup Greek
    yogurt
1 lemon

For the onion, tomato and herb
    salad
2 red onions, peeled and finely
    sliced
juice of 1½ limes
2 large tomatoes
2 large handfuls of coriander
    (cilantro)leaves, finely
    chopped
2 large handfuls of parsley
    leaves, finely chopped
2 tbsp olive oil

1 Preheat the oven to 200°C/400°F/Gas 6 and take the beef out of the fridge to come to room temperature. Put the garlic, paprika, cumin and ground coriander. Add the olive oil and a good pinch of salt and pepper. Squeeze in the juice from the lemon and blend until smooth.

2 Put the beef in a roasting tin, then tip over the paste and rub it all over the beef. Roast for 30–35 minutes until charred on the outside and beautifully tender on the inside.

3 While the beef cooks, start to prepare the raita. Heat the oil in a wok over a high heat and add the pine nuts. Stir-fry for 30 seconds until golden, then remove from the pan and leave to one side. Add the garlic to the pan. Stir-fry for 30 seconds until golden, then add the spinach and a pinch of salt. Continue to stir-fry for 2–3 minutes until the spinach has wilted. Tip the spinach into a fine sieve and leave to drain.

4 Using the back of a spoon, squeeze any excess moisture out of the spinach. Tip into a serving bowl and add the yogurt, then squeeze in the juice from the lemon and season with salt and pepper. Mix well, top with the pine nuts, then cover.

5 To make the salad, put the onions into a mixing bowl and pour over the juice from the limes and add a good pinch of salt. Mix together and leave to one side.

6 Cut the tomatoes for the salad in half and squeeze out the seeds, then finely chop the flesh and put it into the bowl with the onions. Add the chopped herbs to the bowl, pour over the oil and add a pinch of pepper. Mix well.

7 Pop the flatbreads into the oven for 2 minutes to warm through. When the beef is cooked, remove it from the oven and transfer it to a carving board. Slice the beef and serve it with the warm flatbreads, spinach raita and salad. Oh, and a glass or two of red.

MEXICAN STUFFED PEPPERS WITH PECAN SAUCE

1 Preheat the oven to 190°C/375°F/Gas 5. Heat the oil in a large frying pan or skillet over a medium heat, then add the onion and cook, stirring occasionally, for 6–8 minutes, or until the onion has turned golden. Add the minced (ground) beef, garlic, cumin, cloves, chilli flakes, almonds, tomatoes and stock and season with a really good pinch of salt and pepper. Mix well and cook for 10–12 minutes, or until the beef is cooked through and the sauce has reduced down so it's really thick. Throw in the chopped coriander (cilantro) and mix well.

2 Spoon the cooked beef mixture into the pepper halves, drizzle with a little olive oil and bake in the preheated oven for 20–25 minutes, or until the peppers are soft and starting to turn golden brown.

3 Meanwhile, put all the sauce ingredients into a food processor with a splash of water and blend until completely smooth. Drizzle over the sweet, juicy stuffed peppers, sprinkle with a little chopped coriander and serve immediately. Alternatively, serve the sauce on the side, scattered with extra chopped pecans.

SERVES 4
READY IN 1 HOUR

2 tbsp olive oil, plus extra for drizzling
1 large onion, finely chopped
250g/9oz minced (ground) beef
2 garlic cloves, finely chopped
1 tsp ground cumin
¼ tsp ground cloves
½ tsp chilli flakes
25g/1oz/scant ¼ cup almonds, roughly chopped
4 tomatoes, finely chopped
250ml/9fl oz/1 cup beef stock
1 handful coriander (cilantro) leaves, finely chopped, plus extra to serve
2 red (bell) peppers, halved lengthways and deseeded
sea salt and freshly ground black pepper

For the sauce
50g/1¾oz/½ cup pecan nuts, plus extra to serve (optional)
150ml/5fl oz/scant ⅔ cup soured cream

THE BOSPORUS BURGER

SERVES 2
READY IN 15 MINUTES

1 small handful of parsley leaves,
    finely chopped
1 tsp paprika
2 tsp ground cumin
½ tsp ground ginger
½ tsp chilli powder
300g/10½oz minced
    (ground) beef
1 tbsp olive oil
55g/2oz blue cheese
4 tbsp mayonnaise
¼ lemon
2 burger buns
1 handful of mixed lettuce leaves
sea salt

1 Finely chop the parsley and chuck it into a large mixing bowl. Add the paprika, cumin, ground ginger, chilli powder, minced (ground) beef and a really good pinch of salt. Mix everything together really well – I find that squeezing the mix together in your fists works best.

2 Divide the beef mixture into 2 portions and flatten each one into a burger. Push your thumb into the top of each burger to create a little indent, which will help the burgers to cook evenly.

3 Heat the oil in a frying pan or skillet over a high heat and add the burgers, indented side facing up. Cook for 4 minutes, then turn the burgers over, reduce the heat to medium-low and cook for another 3 minutes. Top each burger with half the blue cheese and cook for 1 minute, or until the burgers are cooked through and wonderfully juicy and the cheese has just melted.

4 While the burgers cook, put the mayonnaise in a mixing bowl and squeeze in the juice from the lemon. Add a pinch of salt and mix well. Split the burger buns in half and spread the mayonnaise evenly over the base half of each. Divide the lettuce leaves over the mayo'd buns. Add the cooked burgers, put the top of the buns on the burgers and tuck in straight away.

SUMAC CHICKEN WITH BLACK GREMOLATA & TOMATO SALAD

1 Preheat the oven to 200°C/400°F/Gas 6. Rub a little of the oil over the base of a roasting tin and chuck in the chicken pieces, new potatoes and onion quarters. Smash open the garlic bulb and remove 1 clove for the black gremolata, then scatter the rest over the chicken.

2 Season the chicken with the sumac and thyme, and a good pinch of salt and pepper. Pour over the remaining oil and mix everything together really well. Roast for 35–40 minutes until all the chicken is cooked through and tender, and everything is golden brown.

3 Meanwhile, to make the gremolata, peel the reserved garlic, then chuck it into a mini food processor or blender, and add the olives, chilli, sumac, parsley, dill, oil, balsamic vinegar and a pinch of salt and pepper. Pour over the juice from the lemon and grind into a coarse paste. Tip into a serving bowl and stir in the walnut pieces. Cover and leave to one side to allow those fantastic flavours to intensify.

4 To make the salad, cut the tomatoes into different shapes and sizes, and put them in a serving bowl. Pour in the vinegar and olive oil, then season with the sugar, salt and pepper. Toss together. Cover and leave to one side to allow the tomatoes to soak up the seasonings. Serve the chicken with the potatoes, gremolata and the salad.

SERVES 4
READY IN 45 MINUTES

3 tbsp olive oil
1.5kg/3lb 5oz chicken thighs
    and drumsticks on the bone
500g/1lb 2oz small new
    potatoes
1 red onion, peeled and
    quartered
1 garlic bulb
1 tbsp sumac
2 tsp dried thyme
sea salt and freshly ground
    black pepper

For the black gremolata
85g/3oz/⅔ cup pitted black
    olives
1 dried red chilli
¼ tsp sumac
1 large handful of parsley leaves
1 large handful of dill
3 tbsp olive oil
2 tsp best sticky sweet balsamic
    vinegar
juice of ½ lemon
55g/2oz/scant ½ cup walnut
    pieces

For the tomato salad
300g/10½oz mixed tomatoes,
    such as cherry, vine, baby,
    plum
2 tbsp best sticky sweet
    balsamic vinegar
2 tbsp olive oil
a pinch of sugar

KOREAN BRAISED CHICKEN WITH RICE NOODLES

SERVES 4
READY IN 35 MINUTES

550g/1lb 4oz boneless, skinless chicken thighs
70ml/2¼fl oz/generous ¼ cup soy sauce
1 tbsp oyster sauce
3 tbsp rice wine or dry white wine
½ tbsp sesame oil
2 tbsp brown sugar
½ tsp ground ginger
½ tsp freshly ground black pepper
2 dried red chillies
4 garlic cloves, peeled and crushed
1 onion, peeled and roughly sliced
1 carrot, peeled and sliced into matchsticks
1 courgette (zucchini), sliced
200g/7oz vermicelli rice noodles
100ml/3½fl oz/generous ⅓ cup chicken stock
2 spring onions (scallions), trimmed and finely sliced
½ red chilli, finely sliced
1 small handful of coriander (cilantro) leaves

ALL KOREAN FOOD SHOULD HAVE A BALANCE OF FIVE COLOURS – BLACK, WHITE, YELLOW, GREEN AND RED. HERE, THE BLACK IS FROM THE SOY, THE WHITE FROM THE CHICKEN, YELLOW FROM THE NOODLES, GREEN FROM THE CORIANDER (CILANTRO) AND RED FROM THE CHILLIES.

1 Chuck the chicken in a large, shallow flameproof casserole and pour over the soy sauce, oyster sauce, rice wine, sesame oil, brown sugar, ground ginger and black pepper. Crack open the dried chillies and throw them into the casserole, then add the garlic. Mix everything together really well and heat over a medium heat.

2 Put the onion, carrot and courgette (zucchini) in the casserole with the chicken and mix together. It will look a little dry at this stage, but don't worry – lots of lovely juices will come from the chicken and vegetables. Bring to the boil, cover and reduce the heat to low. Simmer gently for 15 minutes, or until the chicken is just cooked through.

3 Meanwhile, put the noodles in a large mixing bowl, cover with boiling water and leave to one side to soften for about 10 minutes. Pour the stock into a small saucepan and heat gently over a medium-low heat. Once the chicken is cooked, drain the noodles in a colander and add them to the casserole in four little piles. Pour over the stock, then cover and cook for another 10 minutes to allow the noodles to soak up the sauce. Scatter the chilli and spring onions (scallions) over the dish and tear over the coriander (cilantro) leaves, then serve.

CHIMICHURRI CHICKEN WITH RICE & BLACK BEAN SALAD

1 Preheat the oven to 220°C/425°F/Gas 7. Put the chicken on to a chopping board breast-side down. Using a pair of kitchen scissors, cut along either side of the spine from the neck to the rear cavity and remove it. Pull the two sides apart so that the chicken starts to open out, turn it over, breast-side up, and press down hard on each side so that the chicken flattens out.

2 Lay the spatchcocked chicken on a rack over an ovenproof grill pan, rub over the oil and season with salt and pepper. Roast for 35 minutes, or until the chicken is cooked through and its juices run clear.

3 Meanwhile, cook the rice in boiling water for 20–25 minutes until soft, or as directed on the packet.

4 To make the chimichurri, put all the ingredients into a food processor or blender with 100ml/3½fl oz/generous ⅓ cup water and a little salt, and pulse into a coarse paste. Pour into a serving bowl, cover and leave to one side.

5 Put the red onion, mint and parsley into a mini food processor and pulse until finely chopped, then add to a large mixing bowl with the beans. Spoon in one-third of the chimichurri and add the sherry vinegar, then season with salt.

6 Heat a small frying pan or skillet over a medium heat and add the cashew nuts. Toast them until lightly golden, shaking the pan frequently to stop them from burning. Set aside.

7 Tip the salad leaves into a plastic food bag. Squeeze the juice from the lemon into the bag and add the oil. Hold two sides of the bag together, shake well and tip into a serving bowl.

8 Put the roasted chicken on to a carving board. Add the cooked rice and cashew nuts to the bowl with the beans and toss everything together so that the rice is completely coated with the dressing. Serve the lovely hot chicken with the rice and bean salad, the leaf salad and the chimichurri.

SERVES 4
READY IN 45 MINUTES

For the chicken
1 chicken, 1.4kg/3lb 2oz
1 tbsp olive oil
200g/7oz/1 cup brown rice
½ red onion, peeled
1 large handful of mint leaves
1 large handful of parsley leaves
235g/8½oz/generous 1 cup tinned black beans, drained and rinsed
2 tbsp sherry vinegar
100g/3½oz/⅔ cup cashew nuts
sea salt and freshly ground black pepper

For the Chimichurri
1 red chilli, desseded
½ red onion, peeled
2 garlic cloves, peeled
1 large handful of parsley leaves
1 tomato
2 tsp dried oregano
2 tsp ground cumin
1 tsp smoked paprika
4 tbsp olive oil
4 tbsp sherry vinegar

For the leaf salad
120g/4¼oz mixed salad leaves
½ lemon
1 tbsp olive oil

SAFFRON CHICKEN MANSAF

SERVES 4
READY IN 40 MINUTES

350g/12oz/1¾ cups basmati rice
600ml/21fl oz/scant 2½ cups
　chicken stock
¼ tsp saffron threads
2 onions, peeled and finely
　sliced
3 tbsp olive oil
6 cardamom pods
4 garlic cloves, peeled and
　crushed
2 tsp ground cinnamon
3 bay leaves
500g/1lb 2oz boneless, skinless
　chicken thighs
55g/2oz/heaped ⅓ cup pine
　nuts
1 large handful of parsley leaves,
　finely chopped
½ nutmeg
55g/2oz/scant ⅔ cup flaked
　almonds
sea salt and freshly ground
　black pepper
1 bag of green salad, to serve

For the tahini yogurt
300g/10½oz/scant 1¼ cups
　yogurt
2 tbsp tahini
½ lemon

1 Put the rice in a bowl, cover with cold water and stir. Leave to one side for a few minutes to soak and allow the starch to release. Pour the stock into a saucepan and bring to the boil over a medium heat. Once boiled, add the saffron, stir well and remove from the heat.

2 Meanwhile, heat the oil in a large, shallow saucepan over a medium heat and add the onions. Mix well and cook for 4–5 minutes, stirring occasionally, until golden.

3 Crush the cardamon pods by pressing down with the side of a knife, and add them to the cooked onions. Add the garlic, cinnamon, bay leaves and a good pinch of salt. Drain the rice and tip it into the pan. Mix well so that the grains become coated in the oil and spices. Pour over the saffron stock and stir gently. Put the chicken thighs on the top of the rice and poke them down with a spoon. Bring to the boil, cover, reduce the heat to low and cook for 20 minutes, or until the chicken is cooked through and the rice is tender.

4 While the chicken and rice cook, put the pine nuts in a small frying pan or skillet over a medium heat and toast for 4–5 minutes, shaking the pan occasionally, until golden. Remove from the heat and leave to one side.

5 To make the tahini yogurt, tip the yogurt into a serving bowl, add the tahini and a good pinch of salt. Squeeze in the juice from the lemon, mix well and add a grinding of pepper. Leave to one side.

6 Once the saffron mansaf is cooked, grate over the nutmeg and add half the pine nuts, flaked almonds and parsley. Season with salt and pepper, and mix well with a fork. Scatter over the remaining nuts and parsley, and serve with the yogurt and green salad.

JONNY'S DUMPLINGS

SERVES 2
READY IN 15 MINUTES

2 large green savoy cabbage
    leaves
¼ red chilli, deseeded
1 spring onion (scallion),
    trimmed
1 small handful of coriander
    (cilantro) leaves
150g/5½oz raw, peeled king
    prawns (jumbo shrimp)
¼ tsp Chinese five-spice powder
1 tsp light soy sauce, plus extra
    to serve
1 tbsp groundnut (peanut) oil

DIM SUM IS SOMEWHAT OF AN OBSESSION OF MINE. FROM THE SUPER-SLIMY RICE ROLLS TO THE DRY, DELICATE, STEAMED PARCELS OF A HIGH-BROW HONG KONG HOTEL, I CAN'T GET ENOUGH. THE RITUAL OF TICKING THE LITTLE BOXES ON THE MENU, WAITING FOR THE STEAMER TROLLEY AND THEN DIPPING THE GLORY INTO VARIOUS SOY, CHILLI AND VINEGAR CONDIMENTS IS A COMPLETE PLEASURE TO ME. TO MAKE, THOUGH, IT'S NOT SO FUN. HOWEVER, I REALLY WANTED TO GET SOMETHING INTO THIS BOOK, AND AFTER EATING CABBAGE-LEAF DIM SUM AT A RESTAURANT CALLED JONNY'S IN KOREA, I THOUGHT, "BRING IT ON", AND I CAME UP WITH THIS QUICK VERSION.

1 Put the cabbage leaves in a heatproof bowl and cover with boiling water. Leave to soften for 2–3 minutes. Meanwhile, chuck the chilli and spring onion (scallion) into a blender or food processor and add the coriander (cilantro), prawns (shrimp), Chinese five-spice powder and soy sauce. Blend until smooth.

2 Drain the cabbage leaves in a colander and refresh under cold water for a few seconds until they are cool enough to handle. Gently squeeze out any excess water and put on to a chopping board. Cut out the stems and cut the leaves into 2 halves. Put a quarter of the prawn mixture on to each piece of cabbage leaf and roll them up, tucking in the sides. They should look like roundish spring rolls.

3 Heat the oil in a frying pan over a high heat and add the dumplings, fold-side down. Cook for 2 minutes, then pour boiling water into the side of the frying pan to a depth of 2mm/¹⁄₁₆in. Cover, reduce the heat to medium and steam for 4 minutes. Remove the lid and cook for 2–3 minutes until most of the water has evaporated and the dumplings are cooked through. Serve with light soy sauce for dipping.

SIZZLING SEAFOOD

FISH TACOS WITH A SMOKY PAPRIKA & TOMATO SALSA

1 To make the salsa, heat a frying pan or skillet over a high heat until smoking hot. Add the tomatoes, garlic and onion and char on all sides for about 5–6 minutes, or until they are blackened and tender. Remove from the heat. Once cool enough to handle, skin the onion and garlic. Put the tomatoes, garlic, onion, paprika, lime juice, oil and honey into a food processor, season with a good pinch of salt and pepper and blend until lovely and smooth. Pour the salsa back into the frying pan over a medium heat, bring to a gentle boil, then reduce the heat to low and simmer gently, stirring occasionally, for 15 minutes. This will allow all the flavours develop.

2 Heat 2 tablespoons of the oil in a large frying pan over a medium heat and add the fish, skin side down. Cook for 2 minutes, then flip the fillets over, turn off the heat and leave for another 2 minutes to finish cooking.

3 Meanwhile, heat the remaining tablespoon of oil in a small frying pan over a medium heat and add the Parma ham, if using. Fry really quickly, just 10–20 seconds, or until the ham is lovely and crispy. Stir continuously so that it doesn't burn.

4 Flake the fish into a large mixing bowl with the salsa, Parma ham, mozzarella, cherry tomatoes, spring onions (scallions) and cos lettuce. Toss everything together and divide onto the four tortillas. Roll into a cone shape and serve.

SERVES 4
READY IN 35 MINUTES

3 tbsp olive oil

4 red mullet or sea bass fillets, skin on, about 120g/4¼oz each

4 slices Parma ham (optional)

120g/4¼oz mozzarella, finely chopped

8 cherry tomatoes, finely chopped

4 spring onions (scallions), finely chopped

1 cos lettuce, finely chopped

4 corn tortillas

For the salsa

2 tomatoes

2 garlic cloves, unpeeled

1 red onion, unpeeled and cut in half

½ tsp smoked paprika

juice of ½ lime

2 tbsp olive oil

½ tbsp honey

sea salt and freshly ground black pepper

PHUKET SNAPPER WITH HOISIN NOODLES & HERB SALAD

1 Preheat the oven to 200°C/400°F/Gas 6. Oil a piece of foil large enough to wrap up the fish, and put the snapper on top. Finely slice the lemongrass, lime and unpeeled ginger.

2 Spoon the Worcestershire sauce into the cavity of the fish and stuff with the lemongrass, lime and ginger, putting a few slices of lime on the top, if you like. Drizzle over the oil and sprinkle over the black pepper and a good pinch of salt. Wrap the fish tightly in the foil and put in a roasting tin. Roast the fish for 25–30 minutes until cooked through and tender.

3 Meanwhile, make the salad. Put the lemongrass into a mini food processor with the ginger, chilli, fish sauce and sugar, then blend into a smooth paste. Put the onion into a large mixing bowl and pour over the lime juice. Mix well (this will help take the rawness out of the onions). Put the grated carrots over the top.

4 Add the herbs to the salad, followed by the spice paste, then toss together and transfer to a serving bowl. Cover and leave to one side.

5 Cook the noodles in boiling water for 4–5 minutes until soft, or as directed on the packet. Drain and return to the pan. Pour over the hoisin sauce, soy sauce and oil. Mix everything together well and leave to one side. Scatter the peanuts and reserved herb leaves over the salad, and serve with the cooked fish and noodles.

SERVES 4
READY IN 40 MINUTES

1 tbsp groundnut (peanut) oil
2 red snapper (about 500g/1lb 2oz each), cleaned
2 lemongrass stalks, finely sliced
1 lime, finely sliced
5cm/2in piece fresh root ginger, finely sliced
1 tbsp Worcestershire sauce
1 tsp freshly ground black pepper

For the herb salad
2 lemongrass stalks, outer leaves removed
2.5cm/1in piece fresh root ginger, peeled
½ red chilli
2 tbsp fish sauce
1½ tsp sugar
1 red onion, peeled and grated
juice of 1½ limes
300g/10½oz carrots, grated
2 large handfuls of coriander (cilantro) leaves
2 large handfuls of basil leaves, finely chopped
1 large handful of mint leaves, finely chopped
30g/1oz/scant ¼ cup peanuts

For the hoisin noodles
200g/7oz medium egg noodles
3 tbsp hoisin sauce
2 tbsp soy sauce
1 tbsp groundnut (peanut) oil

DONGBAI ROAST COD WITH STIR-FRIED SPINACH & PEANUTS

SERVES 4
READY IN 25 MINUTES

250g/9oz/1¼ cups jasmine rice
2 tsp crushed chilli flakes
2 tbsp sesame seeds
2 tsp cumin seeds
6 tbsp oyster sauce
2 tbsp soy sauce
1 tbsp clear honey
1½ tbsp groundnut (peanut) oil
4 skinless cod fillets (about
    175g/6oz each)

For the spinach and peanuts
1 tbsp chilli oil
55g/2oz/heaped ⅓ cup peanuts
400g/14oz spinach
1 tbsp light soy sauce
2 tsp red wine vinegar

1 Preheat the oven to 200°C/400°F/Gas 6. Cook the rice in boiling water for 10–12 minutes until soft, or as directed on the packet, then drain in a colander. Pour boiling water into the saucepan to a depth of 2.5cm/1in and heat over a low heat. Put the colander with the rice over the pan and leave to steam gently until you are ready to eat.

2 Meanwhile, put half the chilli flakes, sesame seeds and cumin seeds for the roast cod into a spice grinder and grind into a fine powder. Tip into a mixing bowl and add the oyster sauce, soy sauce, honey and 1 tablespoon of the oil, and mix well. Add the fish and mix well so that the fillets are completely coated.

3 Lay the fish in a small roasting tin in a single layer and spoon the remaining marinade over the top. Sprinkle most of the remaining chilli flakes, sesame seeds and cumin seeds over the top, and drizzle over the remaining oil. Roast for 12–15 minutes until the fish is cooked through, tender and flaky.

4 Make the spinach and peanuts while the fish cooks. Heat a wok over a high heat and add the chilli oil and peanuts. Stir-fry for 1 minute, or until just turning golden. Add the spinach and continue to stir-fry for 2–3 minutes until wilted. Drain off the excess moisture and return the wok to a high heat. Pour in the soy sauce and red wine vinegar, and continue to stir-fry for another 1 minute. Sprinkle over the remaining chilli flakes, sesame seeds and cumin seeds. Serve the fish with the sticky rice and the spinach. Remember to spoon over all the lovely juices from the roasting tin, as they are too good to waste.

STEAMED COD IN BANANA LEAF

SERVES 4
READY IN 40 MINUTES

6 tbsp vegetable oil

2 tsp mustard seeds

4 red onions, finely chopped

2 large pinches of dried curry leaves

2 tsp garam masala

juice of 1 lemon

4 large squares banana leaf or baking parchment, about 30 x 30cm/12 x 12in

4 cod fillets, about 150g/5½oz each, skinned

4 fresh curry leaves

4 cocktail sticks

sea salt

THIS IS ANOTHER WONDERFULLY TASTY DISH FROM SOUTH INDIA. FRYING THE FISH IN A BANANA LEAF ADDS A REALLY LOVELY SMOKY FLAVOUR AND KEEPS IN ALL OF THE DELICIOUS JUICES. YOU CAN FIND BANANA LEAVES ONLINE OR IN SPECIALIST SHOPS, BUT IF YOU DON'T WANT TO GO TO THE TROUBLE, USE BAKING PARCHMENT INSTEAD – THE RECIPE WILL WORK JUST AS WELL. YOU CAN MAKE EVERYTHING WELL IN ADVANCE AND JUST COOK THE PARCELS BEFORE SERVING.

1 Heat 4 tablespoons of the oil in a frying pan or skillet over a medium-low heat, then chuck in the mustard seeds. Let them crackle for 30 seconds, then add the onions and cook, stirring occasionally, for 10–12 minutes, or until they are really golden and sticky. Rub the dried curry leaves between your hands so that they break up, then scatter over the onions. Add the garam masala and lemon juice and season with a good pinch of salt. Mix well and cook for a further minute.

2 Spoon a heaped tablespoon of the cooked onion mixture onto the middle of a banana leaf, then use the back of the spoon to spread the onion so it's just wide enough for one of the fish fillets to sit on top. Place the cod fillets on top of the onion mix, then spread another heaped spoonful of the onion mixture over and top with a curry leaf. Wrap the fish in the banana leaf like a parcel, tucking in the sides, and fasten the top with a cocktail stick. Repeat with the remaining pieces of fish and banana leaf.

3 Add the remaining 2 tablespoons of oil to any remaining onion mixture in the frying pan and heat over a low-medium heat. Add the fish parcels and then cook for 16–18 minutes, or until the fish is cooked through and tender.

4 Serve immediately, still wrapped in the banana leaf so there is no risk of losing any of the delicious juices.

MEXICAN SEA BREAM WITH ROASTED LEMON COURGETTES & SPICY LIME SEASONING

1 Preheat the oven to 200°C/400°F/Gas 6. To make the lemon courgettes, put the courgettes (zucchini) in a roasting tin with the thyme, olive oil and a good pinch of salt and pepper. Pour over the juice from the lemon and mix everything together well. Roast for 30–35 minutes until tender and creamy.

2 Meanwhile, soak the chipotle chillies in 2 tablespoons hot water and leave to one side. Heat a non-stick frying pan or skillet over a high heat. Carefully put the onion and garlic into the hot pan and toast for 2 minutes. Add the tomatoes and turn the garlic. Cook for another 2–3 minutes until the tomatoes and onion are charred on the cooked side and the garlic is charred on both sides.

3 While the tomatoes are charring, combine lime zest, chilli flakes and salt for the spicy seasoning in a serving bowl. Leave to one side.

4 Transfer the charred ingredients and the chipotle chillies with their soaking liquid to a blender or food processor, and add the cinnamon, paprika, brown sugar, thyme and a good pinch of salt. Squeeze in the juice of 1½ of the limes used for the spicy seasoning and blend into a smooth sauce.

5 Pour the sauce into a large, shallow saucepan and bring to the boil over a medium heat. Cook for 10 minutes, stirring occasionally, then add the fish fillets, skin-side down, to the hot sauce. Cover and cook for 4–5 minutes until the fish is beautifully tender and flaky. Pinch the spicy seasoning mixture between your fingers to accentuate all the flavours while the fish cooks. Cut the remaining lime half into 4 segments.

6 Scatter the coriander (cilantro) over the cooked fish and drizzle over the extra virgin olive oil. Serve the fish with the cooked courgettes, tortillas, lime segments and the spicy lime seasoning.

SERVES 4
READY IN 40 MINUTES

2 chipotle chillies
1 red onion, peeled and quartered
4 garlic cloves, peeled
4 tomatoes
1 tsp ground cinnamon
½ tsp paprika
1 tsp brown sugar
leaves from 1 large thyme sprig
4 sea bream fillets (about 125g/4½oz each)
1 handful of coriander (cilantro) leaves
2 tbsp best-quality extra virgin olive oil
4 large flour tortillas, to serve

For the lemon courgettes
600g/1lb 5oz courgettes (zucchini), cut into 1.5cm/⅝in chunks
3 large thyme sprigs
2 tbsp olive oil
juice of ½ lemon
sea salt and freshly ground black pepper

For the spicy lime seasoning
zest and juice 2 limes
1 tsp crushed chilli flakes
1 tsp sea salt

PRAWN TORTAS
WITH SALSA MEXICANA

SERVES 2
READY IN 20 MINUTES

200g/7oz unpeeled potatoes,
   chopped into 1cm/½in cubes
1 garlic clove, peeled
4 spring onions (scallions),
   trimmed
1 handful of coriander (cilantro)
   leaves
175g/6oz raw, peeled king
   prawns (jumbo shrimp)
30g/1oz feta cheese
½ egg
80g/2¾oz/scant ⅔ cup plain
   (all-purpose) flour
1 tbsp olive oil, plus extra for
   greasing
sea salt and freshly ground black
   pepper

For the salsa Mexicana
1 garlic clove, peeled
100g/3½oz/⅔ cup drained
   sun-dried tomatoes in oil
1 dried chipotle chilli
1 tbsp olive oil
juice of ½ lime

1 Cook the potatoes in a saucepan of boiling water for
8 minutes, or until tender. Drain in a colander and refresh
under cold water, then drain again. Return the potatoes
to the saucepan and lightly mash them so that they start
to break down. Leave to one side.

2 While the potatoes cook, put the garlic and spring onions
(scallions) into a food processor with the coriander (cilantro)
and blend to roughly chop. Add the prawns (jumbo shrimp)
and feta cheese, and blend into a rough paste. Tip the paste
into a large mixing bowl, add the egg and flour, then season
with salt and pepper. Transfer the mashed potatoes to
the bowl and mix everything together well until a dough-
like consistency.

3 Heat the oil in a small frying pan or skillet over a high heat.
Scoop the potato mixture into the pan and spread it out
to cover the base. Reduce the heat to medium and cook
for 1½–2 minutes, shaking the pan occasionally, until golden
on one side.

4 Meanwhile, to make the salsa, put the garlic, sun-dried
tomatoes, chilli and oil into a mini food processor or blender.
Pour in the lime juice, season with salt and blend into
a smooth paste. Tip the smoky salsa into a serving bowl
and leave to one side.

5 When the tortas has cooked on one side, rub a little oil over
a side plate and carefully place it, oil-side down, over the pan
with the half-cooked tortas. Holding the plate and the frying
pan handle, carefully flip the pan over so that the tortas rests
on the plate. Slip it back into the pan and cook for another
1½–2 minutes until golden. Serve with the hot, smoky salsa.

PRAWN & HERB BREWAT

1 Heat the oil in a large saucepan over a medium heat. Add the onion and garlic and stir-fry for 4–5 minutes until golden.

2 Add the cherry tomatoes, passata, honey, cumin, paprika, chilli powder, black pepper and a good pinch of salt to the cooked onion. Pour in the lemon juice and add the stock. Mix everything together really well, then bring to the boil. Cover and reduce the heat to low. Cook for 10 minutes, stirring occasionally, to allow the sauce to develop in flavour.

3 When the sauce has cooked, turn the heat up to medium and add the prawns (jumbo shrimp) and the chopped coriander (cilantro) leaves and stalks. Cook for 5–6 minutes, stirring occasionally, until the prawns have cooked through and turned pink.

4 While the prawns cook, cook the noodles in boiling water for 2–3 minutes until soft, or as directed on the packet. Drain and return them to the pan. Add the oil, the chopped coriander leaves, the cumin, chilli powder and a good pinch of salt and pepper. Squeeze in the juice from the lemon and mix everything together well so that all the spices and dressing completely coat the yummy noodles. Serve with the cooked prawn and herb brewat.

SERVES 4
READY IN 30 MINUTES

2 tbsp olive oil
1 red onion, peeled and finely chopped
4 garlic cloves, peeled and finely chopped
200g/7oz/heaped 1⅓ cups cherry tomatoes, halved
250g/9oz/1 cup tomato passata
1 tsp clear honey
2 tsp ground cumin
1 tsp paprika
½ tsp chilli powder
½ tsp freshly ground black pepper
juice of ½ lemon
100ml/3½fl oz/generous ⅓ cup vegetable stock
1 large handful of coriander (cilantro), roughly chopped
500g/1lb 2oz raw, peeled king prawns (jumbo shrimp) (with or without tails)

For the rice noodles
1 large handful of coriander (cilantro) leaves, roughly chopped
200g/7oz vermicelli rice noodles
2 tbsp olive oil
½ tsp ground cumin
¼ tsp chilli powder
½ lemon
sea salt and freshly ground black pepper

COCHIN CRAB CAKES

SERVES 2
READY IN 15 MINUTES

2 tbsp groundnut (peanut) oil

1 tsp mustard seeds

a large pinch of dried curry
   leaves

¼ tsp turmeric

½ tsp chilli powder

3 spring onions (scallions),
   trimmed and finely chopped

5 cherry tomatoes, finely
   chopped

1 handful of coriander (cilantro)
   leaves, finely chopped

200g/7oz/1½ cups cooked
   white crab meat

60g/2¼oz/¾ cup fresh
   breadcrumbs

1 small egg

1 lime

sea salt

MY COCHIN CRAB CAKES MAKE THE PERFECT LIGHT MEAL.
THEY ARE PACKED WITH JUICY CRAB, AND WITH TOMATOES,
CORIANDER AND SPRING ONIONS TO FRESHEN THINGS UP.
FINALLY, MUSTARD SEEDS, CURRY LEAVES, TURMERIC AND
CHILLI ADD THE FLAVOURS OF SOUTH INDIA. THE HIT OF LIME
AT THE END ACCENTUATES ALL THE SPICES EVEN MORE,
SO IN ONLY 15 MINUTES YOU GET SOMETHING AMAZING.

1 Heat 1 tablespoon of the oil in a small frying pan or skillet
over a medium heat and add the mustard seeds. Fry for
30 seconds, shaking the pan continuously, or until the
mustard seeds start popping. Rub the curry leaves between
your hands so that they break into the pan, then remove
the pan from the heat. Add the turmeric and chilli powder,
and leave to one side.

2 Put the spring onions (scallions), cherry tomatoes and
coriander (cilantro) into a mixing bowl. Tip in the crab and
breadcrumbs, and season with salt. Add the cooked spices
and oil from the frying pan, then crack in the egg and mix
everything together well. Divide the mixture into 4 and
flatten each one into a crab cake about 1cm/½in thick.

3 Heat the remaining oil in a large frying pan or skillet over
a medium heat and fry the crab cakes for 2 minutes on
each side, or until beautifully golden and warmed through.
Cut the lime into wedges and serve with the hot crab cakes.

SCALLOP CEVICHE WITH NOODLES & AVOCADO SALAD

1 Put the peanuts and in a frying pan or skillet and toast over a medium heat for 4–5 minutes, shaking the pan occasionally, until golden. Remove from the heat and set aside to cool.

2 Divide the chopped chilli and spring onions (scallions) evenly between 2 bowls, one for the ceviche and one for the noodles.

3 Cook the noodles in boiling water until soft, as directed on the packet. While the noodles cook, cut the scallops into thin slices on the horizontal and lay them in an even layer in a shallow serving dish. Pour over the lime juice and shake the dish so that all the scallops are coated. Cover and leave to one side for 8–10 minutes so that the scallops can "cook" in the acid. Remember to shake the dish from time to time.

4 When the noodles have cooked, drain in a colander and refresh under cold water and drain again. Return them to the pan and dress with the soy sauce, olive oil and sesame oil. Mix well, then tip the noodles into a serving bowl. Scatter with the one bowl of the chilli and spring onions, cover and leave to one side.

5 Make the dressing for the salad by whisking the red wine vinegar and sugar until the sugar dissolves. Pour in the oils, then add the coriander and a pinch of salt. Whisk together well.

6 Scoop out small pieces of the avocado flesh using a teaspoon and put them into the bowl with the dressing. Mix everything together so that the avocado does not discolour. Tip on to a serving plate and scatter over the pumpkin seeds. Set aside.

7 Add the fish sauce to the "cooked" scallops, then add the sugar and the remaining chilli and spring onions, and lemongrass, and toss together. Rip the mint leaves over the top, scatter over the toasted peanuts and serve with the noodles and avocado salad.

SERVES 4
READY IN 30 MINUTES

30g/1oz/scant ¼ cup peanuts, roughly chopped
2 lemongrass stalks, trimmed, outer leaves removed and finely chopped
6 spring onions (scallions), trimmed and finely chopped
1 red chilli, finely chopped
200g/7oz buckwheat noodles
375g/13oz scallops
juice of 2 limes
3 tbsp soy sauce
2 tbsp olive oil
1 tsp sesame oil
2 tbsp fish sauce
1 tsp sugar
1 large handful of mint leaves

For the avocado salad
2 tbsp red wine vinegar
2 tsp sugar
2 tbsp olive oil
1 tsp sesame oil
1 tsp ground coriander
2 ripe avocados, halved and stones removed
1 tbsp pumpkin seeds
sea salt

SEA BASS CEVICHE

250g/9oz very fresh firm sea
   bass fillets, skinned and very
   thinly sliced
juice of 4 limes
2 tomatoes
1 red chilli, deseeded and finely
   chopped
2 large handfuls coriander
   (cilantro) leaves, roughly
   chopped
1 red onion, finely chopped
½ small cos lettuce, finely sliced
2 tbsp olive oil
sea salt and freshly ground black
   pepper

CEVICHE IS A DELICIOUS, REFRESHING DISH THAT IS SERVED ALL OVER THE COAST OF MEXICO AND SOUTH AMERICA. THE FISH 'COOKS' IN THE LIME JUICE, WITHOUT USING ANY HEAT, SO YOU REALLY HAVE TO USE THE FRESHEST FISH YOU CAN BUY. DON'T USE ANYTHING THAT'S BEEN FROZEN.

1 Spread the sea bass slices out in a shallow dish, add the lime juice and season with a really good pinch of salt. Turn the pieces over, and continue turning them, until the fish is completely coated. Leave to marinate, stirring occasionally, for 15–20 minutes, or until the flesh has turned opaque.

2 Meanwhile, cut the tomatoes in half, squeeze out the pips and finely chop the flesh. This is so the ceviche isn't watery.

3 Put the marinated fish and all its juices in a large mixing bowl with the tomatoes, red chilli, coriander (cilantro), onion, cos lettuce, oil and a really good pinch of pepper. Gently mix together and serve immediately.

SALMON BIBIMBAP

BIBIMBAP IS A CLASSIC KOREAN RICE DISH. COOKED
RICE IS PUT INTO A BOILING-HOT STONE BOWL, SO THAT IT
FORMS A CRUNCHY BASE. DIFFERENT TOPPINGS – SALMON,
EGGS, VEGETABLES OR PORK – ARE ADDED, AND THE DISH
IS SERVED WITH KIMCHI AND A SOY-BASED SAUCE. TO GET
THAT CRISPY BASE, MAKE SURE, WHEN YOU COOK MY SALMON
VERSION, THAT THE PAN IS REALLY HOT BEFORE YOU ADD THE
COOKED RICE.

SERVES 2
READY IN 20 MINUTES

120g/4¼oz/scant ⅔ cup
   jasmine rice
2 tbsp olive oil
2 boneless, skinless salmon
   fillets
1cm/½in piece fresh root ginger,
   peeled and finely chopped
3 spring onions (scallions),
   trimmed and finely chopped
1 tbsp light soy sauce
1 tbsp cider vinegar
2 eggs
1 tsp sesame seeds

For the chilli dressing
1 garlic clove, peeled
4 tbsp chilli sauce
1 tbsp soy sauce
1 tbsp cider vinegar
1 tsp sesame oil

1 Cook the rice in boiling water for 10–12 minutes until soft,
or as directed on the packet. Drain in a colander, return to
the pan, then cover and leave to one side. Meanwhile, heat
1 tablespoon of the oil for the salmon in a frying pan or skillet
over a medium heat and add the salmon. Cook for 2 minutes,
then turn, reduce the heat to low and cook for 1½–2 minutes
until cooked on the outside and pink in the centre. Leave to
one side.

2 While the salmon cooks put all the dressing ingredients into
a mini food processor, and blend until smooth. Set aside.

3 Add the ginger, sping onions (scallions), soy sauce and cider
vinegar to the rice, then mix together really well using a fork.
Cover and leave to one side.

4 Heat the remaining oil in a large frying pan or skillet over a
high heat and add the rice, spreading it evenly, then create
two wells, using a spoon, and crack in the eggs. Cover and
cook for 2–3 minutes until the whites have set, the yolks are
runny and the rice has started to brown underneath. Divide
the rice and eggs between two plates. Flake over the salmon
and scatter over the sesame seeds. Drizzle with the dressing
and serve.

VERACRUZ RICE

SERVES 4
READY IN 40 MINUTES

2 tbsp olive oil
1 onion, finely chopped
400g/14oz/scant 1⅔ cups
    tinned chopped tomatoes
1 red chilli, deseeded and finely
    chopped
2 garlic cloves, peeled and
    crushed
5cm/2in cinnamon stick
3 cloves
½ tsp sugar
350g/12oz/1¾ cups basmati rice
600ml/21fl oz/scant 2½ cups
    chicken or vegetable stock
8 raw large king prawns (jumbo
    shrimp), shells on
1 handful coriander (cilantro)
    leaves, roughly chopped
juice of 1 lime
sea salt and freshly ground black
    pepper
1 lime, quartered, to serve

1 Heat the oil in a large frying or skillet over a medium heat, then add the onion and fry, stirring occasionally, for 6–8 minutes or until the onion has turned golden. Add the tomatoes, red chilli, garlic, cinnamon, cloves and sugar and season with a good pinch of salt and pepper. Mix well and bring to the boil, then cover, reduce the heat to low and simmer gently for 10 minutes.

2 Meanwhile, put the rice into a large saucepan, cover with cold water and stir, then set aside for 5 minutes to soak. Tip the rice into a colander and give it a really good rinse under cold water, until the water coming out of the rice runs clear. This washes the starch out of the rice and makes sure you get lovely, separated grains.

3 Tip the washed rice back into the saucepan and place over a medium heat. Add the tomatoes and hot stock and gently mix together. Bring to the boil, then cover, reduce the heat to low and simmer for 2 minutes.

4 Place the prawns (jumbo shrimp) on top of the rice, put the lid back on the saucepan and cook for a further 10–12 minutes, or until all the water is absorbed and the rice is almost cooked but still has some bite. Remove from the heat and remove the lid. Place a clean tea towel over the rice, then replace the lid and set aside to steam for 5–10 minutes.

5 Remove the cooked prawns from the rice and set aside. Add the coriander (cilantro) and lime juice to the rice, season with a really good pinch of salt and pepper and mix well. Place the prawns back on the rice and serve immediately with the lime wedges.

VIBRANT VEGGIES

FALAFEL DIPPERS

SERVES 4
READY IN 1 HOUR

½ red onion, roughly chopped
½ green chilli, deseeded and
    roughly chopped
2 garlic cloves
1 large handful mint leaves, plus
    extra to serve
400g/14oz tinned chickpeas,
    washed and drained
1 tsp ground cumin
2 tbsp flour
juice and zest of 1 lemon
4 tbsp sesame seeds
2 tbsp olive oil
sea salt and freshly ground black
    pepper

For the dip
200ml/7fl oz/scant 1 cup
    natural yogurt
3 tbsp tahini paste
juice of ½ lemon

1 Put the onion, green chilli, garlic and mint into a food processor and pulse for a few seconds until everything is finely chopped. Add the chickpeas, cumin, flour, lemon juice and zest and season with a really good pinch of salt and pepper. Blitz the lot into a fairly smooth paste, tip into a bowl, cover and refrigerate for 30 minutes.

2 To make the dip, mix the yogurt, tahini paste and lemon juice in a bowl, season with a good pinch of salt and pepper and set aside.

3 Divide the falafel mixture into eight and mould into burger shapes. Scatter the sesame seeds onto a plate and press a burger into the sesame seeds until coated on all sides. Repeat with the remaining burgers.

4 Heat the oil in a frying pan over a medium heat, then fry the falafel for 3 minutes on each side, or until golden and crispy. Serve immediately with the dip and a scattering of mint leaves.

HUEVOS MEXICANOS

TO LEARN ABOUT REAL MEXICAN FOOD YOU HAVE TO GO
AND STAY WITH MY WONDERFUL FRIEND ESTELLA AT HER
BEAUTIFUL CASA IN THE ROLLING HILLS OF PUEBLA. SHE IS
SUCH A CHARACTER; SO PASSIONATE ABOUT MEXICAN FOOD
AND ALWAYS WEARING A CHEEKY SMILE ON HER FACE. ON
THE FIRST MORNING AT ESTELLA'S CASA, SHE GAVE ME MY
FIRST TASTE OF REAL MEXICAN FOOD – HUEVOS MEXICANOS
– WHICH SHE SERVED WITH WARM TORTILLAS. I STAYED WITH
MY FRIEND FOR A WEEK, DURING WHICH TIME SHE TAUGHT
ME MY TOMATILLOS FROM MY TAMALES, MY CHILLI POBLANOS
FROM MY SERRANOS AND SHE PASSED ON HER PASSION FOR
REAL MEXICAN COOKING.

SERVES 2
READY IN 20 MINUTES

2 tbsp vegetable oil
1 small red onion, finely
   chopped
½ red (bell) pepper, deseeded
   and finely chopped
1 garlic clove, finely chopped
½ green chilli, deseeded and
   finely chopped
2 tomatoes, finely chopped
4 large eggs, beaten
2 spring onions (scallions),
   finely chopped
1 small handful coriander
   (cilantro) leaves
sea salt and freshly ground
   black pepper

1 Heat the oil in a large frying pan or skillet over a medium
heat, then add the onion, red (bell) pepper, garlic and green
chilli. Cook, stirring occasionally, for 6–8 minutes, or until
the onion has turned golden. Add the tomatoes, mix well and
cook for a further 3–4 minutes, or until the tomatoes have
started to soften.

2 Tip in the eggs and season with a good pinch of salt and
pepper. Mix well and leave for a minute or so, or until the
eggs begin to set round the edge of the pan, then mix
everything around until the eggs have set completely.

3 Throw in the spring onions (scallions) and coriander (cilantro),
give the scrambled eggs one final mix and serve immediately.

CHEESE QUESADILLAS WITH GREEN MOLE SAUCE

SERVES 4
READY IN 1 HOUR

8 large flour tortillas
300g/10½oz mozzarella, thinly
    sliced

For the green mole sauce
2 large handfuls parsley leaves
2 large handfuls coriander
    (cilantro) leaves
2 large mild green chillies,
    deseeded
4 spring onions (scallions)
juice of 2 limes
30g/1oz/scant ¼ cup pumpkin
    seeds
50g/1¾oz/⅓ cup sesame seeds
2 garlic cloves
½ tbsp cumin seeds
2 tbsp olive oil
560ml/19¼fl oz/2¼ cups hot
    vegetable stock
sea salt and freshly ground black
    pepper

1 To make the green mole sauce, put all the ingredients into a food processor, season with a really good pinch of salt and pepper and blend on a high setting for about 5 minutes, or until really smooth. Pour into a large saucepan and bring to the boil. Cover, reduce the heat to low and simmer gently, stirring occasionally, for 30 minutes until the sauce has reduced slightly and the flavours have developed. The sauce will start to look a little grainy at this point, so pour back into the blender and blend for 30 seconds until beautifully smooth again. If using an upright blender, remember to leave a tiny gap in the lid so that the steam can escape.

2 Heat a large frying pan or skillet over a medium heat and put in one of the tortillas. Lay a quarter of the mozzarella over the tortilla, then put another one over the top. Heat for about 2 minutes, or until the cheese starts to bubble out of the sides of the quesadillas and the bottom tortilla has started to go crispy. Push the top of the quesadilla down with a spatula and then flip it over. Cook for another 2 minutes, or until the tortilla is crispy. Repeat with the other tortillas.

3 Cut each quesadilla into quarters and serve immediately with the Green Mole Sauce.

INDIAN SPINACH CUTLETS WITH RAITA

1 Put the potatoes in a large saucepan of water. Place over a high heat, bring to the boil, then turn the heat down and simmer for 15–20 minutes until tender. While the potatoes are cooking, place the spinach in a colander on top to steam for 8–10 minutes until completely wilted.

2 Drain the potatoes and mash until smooth. Once the spinach has cooled, squeeze out the excess moisture with your hands. This will stop the cutlets from being soggy.

3 Heat 2 tablespoons of the oil in a frying pan or skillet over a medium heat, then stir-fry the onion, ginger and green chilli for 4–5 minutes until soft. Chuck in the pepper, garam masala and salt and cook for a further minute, then remove from the heat and set aside to cool.

4 Meanwhile, mix the raita ingredients together in a bowl, season with a good pinch of salt and pepper and set aside to cool.

5 Once everything has cooled to room temperature, put the mashed potato, spinach, onion mixture and flour in a bowl, mix well, cover and set aside for 30 minutes.

6 Divide the mixture into four parts and shape each one into a flattened cutlet. Spread the breadcrumbs out on a plate and gently press a cutlet into the breadcrumbs until coated on all sides. Repeat with the remaining cutlets.

7 Heat the remaining 2 tablespoons of oil in a frying pan over a medium heat, then fry the cutlets for 2–3 minutes on each side, or until golden and crispy. Serve immediately with the raita, sprinkled with ground cumin.

SERVES 4
READY IN 1 HOUR 20 MINUTES

200g/7oz potatoes, peeled and cut into large chunks
400g/14oz spinach, washed
4 tbsp vegetable oil
1 large onion, finely chopped
2.5cm/1in piece root ginger, peeled and finely chopped
1 green chilli, deseeded and finely chopped
1½ tsp freshly ground black pepper
1 tsp garam masala
1 tsp sea salt
2 tbsp plain (all-purpose) flour
2 large handfuls dried breadcrumbs

For the raita
250ml/9fl oz/1 cup natural yogurt
½ cucumber, deseeded and very finely chopped
juice of ½ lemon
1 small handful mint leaves
ground cumin, to serve
sea salt and freshly ground black pepper

WARM AUBERGINE SALAD

SERVES 2
READY IN 15 MINUTES

5 tbsp olive oil

2 tsp dried mint

2 aubergines (eggplants), sliced
  into 5mm/¼ in rings

½ red onion

1½ lemons

½ red chilli

100g/3½oz/heaped ⅔ cup
  cherry tomatoes

75g/2½oz/scant ⅔ cup pitted
  black olives

2 large handfuls of parsley
  leaves

½ tsp sumac

1 tsp ground cumin

2 tbsp pine nuts (optional)

sea salt and freshly ground black
  pepper

1 Preheat the grill (broiler) to high. Meanwhile, put 3 tablespoons of the oil, 1½ teaspoons of the mint and a good pinch of salt in a mixing bowl, and mix well. Brush both sides of the aubergine (eggplant) rings with the seasoned oil. Put the aubergines on to a grill rack and grill (broil) for 5–6 minutes until golden on one side.

2 While the aubergines cook, peel and finely slice the onion, then chuck it in a large mixing bowl. Squeeze over the juice from the lemons, add a pinch of salt and mix well. Finely chop the chilli and cut the cherry tomatoes in half. Put them in the bowl with the onion.

3 When the aubergines have cooked on one side, turn them over and grill for another 5–6 minutes until golden on the other side and tender in the centre.

4 Tear the olives and rip the parsley leaves into the mixing bowl with the salad. Add the remaining oil and mint, and the sumac, cumin and a good pinch of black pepper. Toss everything together. Put the cooked aubergines in the bowl with the salad and mix everything together really well. Serve the salad with the pine nuts, if using, scattered over the top.

ROASTED VEGETABLES WITH CHILLI TAPENADE

1 Preheat the oven to 200°C/400°F/Gas 6. Put the prepared onions, (bell) peppers, courgettes (zucchini) and aubergine (eggplant) in a roasting tin. Pour over the olive oil, then add the thyme and a good pinch of salt and pepper. Mix everything together really well and roast for 25 minutes, or until the vegetables are almost cooked through.

2 While the vegetables are cooking, make the chilli tapenade. Put the garlic, olives, anchovies, parsley, chilli powder, cumin, oil and a pinch of salt and pepper into a blender or food processor. Pour over the lemon juice and blend into a coarse paste. Tip into a serving bowl, cover and leave to one side for the savoury flavours to develop.

3 When the vegetables have almost cooked, remove from the oven and put the tomatoes over the top. Cook for another 8–10 minutes until all the vegetables are tender and golden and the tomatoes have just started to break down. Pop the bread into the oven for the last 5 minutes to warm through.

4 Put the pine nuts into a small frying pan or skillet over a medium heat and toast for 2–3 minutes, shaking the pan occasionally, until golden. Remove from the heat and leave to one side. Strip the mint leaves from the stems. Pour the lemon juice over the cooked vegetables, crumble over the feta cheese and rip over the mint. Scatter over the toasted pine nuts, then serve with the chilli tapenade and warm bread.

SERVES 4
READY IN 45 MINUTES

2 red onions, peeled and cut into bite-sized pieces
2 red (bell) peppers, deseeded and cut into bite-sized pieces
2 courgettes (zucchini), cut into bite-sized pieces
1 aubergine (eggplant), cut into bite-sized pieces
3 tbsp olive oil
1 tbsp dried thyme
250g/9oz/heaped 1¾ cups cherry tomatoes on the vine
1 loaf of fabulously crusty bread
55g/2oz/heaped ⅓ cup pine nuts
2 large handfuls of mint leaves
juice of ½ lemon
100g/3½oz feta cheese
sea salt and freshly ground black pepper

For the chilli tapenade
1 garlic clove, peeled
85g/3oz/⅔ cup pitted black olives
4 anchovy fillets
1 large handful of parsley leaves
¼ tsp chilli powder
1½ tsp ground cumin
2 tbsp olive oil
juice of ½ lemon

GRILLED HALLOUMI, SUNDRIED TOMATOES & OLIVES

SERVES 4
READY IN 15 MINUTES

250g/9oz halloumi, cut into
5mm/¼in thick slices
50g/1¾oz/⅓ cup pine nuts
250g/9oz cherry tomatoes
100g/3½oz/heaped ¾ cup
pitted black olives, roughly
chopped
2 large handfuls basil leaves,
roughly torn
100g/3½oz/1 cup sun-dried
tomatoes in oil, drained and
finely chopped
juice of 1 lemon
¼ tsp chilli flakes
1 tbsp olive oil, plus extra for
dressing (optional)
sea salt and freshly ground
black pepper

THIS IS ADAPTED FROM A SALAD I HAD IN ISTANBUL, WHERE THEY USE WONDERFUL TURKISH CHILLIES THAT HAVE A MILD, SMOKY, SUN-DRIED TASTE. I FOUND THAT BY MIXING SUN-DRIED TOMATOES AND CHILLI FLAKES YOU CAN CREATE A SIMILAR FLAVOUR.

1 Heat a griddle pan over a high heat until smoking, then griddle the halloumi pieces for about 30 seconds on each side, or until you can see lovely charred lines. Remove from the heat and set aside.

2 Heat a small frying pan or skillet over a medium heat. Add the pine nuts and gently toast for 1–2 minutes, or until the pine nuts are golden brown. They will change colour very suddenly, so watch them carefully, and every now and then, shake the pan so the nuts move about and don't burn. Transfer the pine nuts to a plate to cool.

3 Cut the cherry tomatoes into different shapes and sizes: lengthways, sideways, quarters and leave some whole. This will make the salad look amazing and more interesting to eat. Put them in a large mixing bowl with the olives, basil, sun-dried tomatoes, lemon juice, chilli flakes and half the toasted pine nuts. Season with a small pinch of salt and good pinch of pepper and mix well. There should be enough oil in the sun-dried tomatoes to coat everything. If not, stir in extra olive oil.

4 To serve, heap the cherry tomatoes in a large serving bowl and scatter over the remaining pine nuts. Top the salad with the grilled halloumi, then drizzle over a tablespoon of olive oil. Serve immediately with the squeezed lemon halves.

BLACK PEPPER & SOY AUBERGINES

1 Heat the oil in a large frying pan or skillet over a medium heat and add the aubergine (eggplant) wedges, stirring well to make sure all the pieces are coated in the oil. Cook, stirring occasionally, for 6 minutes and then add the garlic. Continue to cook for 2 minutes, or until the aubergine is tender and cooked through and the garlic is just turning golden. Stir in the tomato purée (paste), soy sauce, sugar, pepper and lime juice, and cook for 1 minute.

2 Transfer to a large mixing bowl and add the onion, cherry tomatoes, green (bell) pepper and red chilli. Toss together and serve immediately.

SERVES 4
READY IN 15 MINUTES

4 tbsp vegetable oil

1 aubergine (eggplant), cut into wedges about 1.5cm/⅝in-thick wedges

1 garlic clove

1 tbsp tomato purée (paste)

2 tbsp soy sauce

a pinch of sugar

1 tsp freshly ground black pepper

juice of ½ lime

½ red onion, finely chopped

100g/3½oz cherry tomatoes, cut into quarters

1 green (bell) pepper, deseeded and finely chopped

½ red chilli, deseeded and finely chopped

CAMBODIAN GINGER & COCONUT AUBERGINES

SERVES 4
READY IN 1 HOUR

1 tbsp vegetable oil

2 large aubergines (eggplants)

2 tbsp desiccated coconut

5cm/2in piece root ginger, peeled and finely sliced

500ml/17fl oz/2 cups coconut cream

2 tbsp oyster sauce

1 tsp freshly ground black pepper

a large pinch of sugar

4 spring onions (scallions), finely sliced

LIKE MANY CAMBODIAN DISHES, THESE AUBERGINES (EGGPLANTS) HAVE A MIX OF THAI AND CHINESE FLAVOURS. IT WORKS BEAUTIFULLY, WITH THE TENDER CHUNKS OF ROASTED AUBERGINE SOAKING UP THE CREAMY COCONUT SAUCE. THE MAIN SPICE HERE IS BLACK PEPPER, WHICH IS OFTEN USED IN CAMBODIAN COOKING INSTEAD OF CHILLI – ADD AN EXTRA HALF TEASPOON IF YOU WANT AN EXTRA KICK.

1 Preheat the oven to 200°C/400°F/Gas 6. Rub the oil over the skin of the aubergines (eggplants), transfer to a roasting tray and roast for 25–30 minutes, or until soft but not cooked to a pulp. Once cool enough to handle, peel off the skin and chop the soft flesh into large chunks.

2 Heat a shallow frying pan over a medium heat, then add the desiccated coconut and ginger. Cook for 2–3 minutes, stirring continuously, until the coconut starts turning golden. Pour in the coconut cream, oyster sauce, black pepper and sugar and mix well. Bring to the boil and add the cooked aubergine. Reduce the heat to low and simmer for 5 minutes until the aubergine is warmed through and the sauce slightly reduced. Scatter over the spring onions (scallions) and serve immediately.

BEIRUT RATATOUILLE

1 Heat the oil in a large saucepan over a medium heat and add the onion and garlic, and mix well. Add the mushrooms to the pan, mix everything together and cook for 3–4 minutes, stirring occasionally, until the mushrooms have cooked down.

2 Add the (bell) peppers, aubergine (eggplant) and courgette (zucchini) to the pan with the cooked mushrooms, then add the chickpeas, tomato purée (paste), tinned tomatoes, cumin, paprika, chilli powder, black pepper and a really good pinch of salt.

3 Pour in 320ml/11fl oz/scant 1⅓ cups boiling water and mix well. Increase the heat to high and bring to the boil. Cover, leaving a slight gap to allow the excess steam to escape, then reduce the heat to medium and simmer for 25–30 minutes, stirring occasionally, until the vegetables are cooked through but still have a little bite.

4 Tip the salad into a serving bowl. Just before serving, mix the chopped parsley into the ratatouille. Serve with the lemon wedges and the mixed salad.

SERVES 4
READY IN 45 MINUTES

2 tbsp olive oil

1 red onion, peeled and finely chopped

4 garlic cloves, peeled and finely chopped

150g/5½oz button mushrooms, roughly sliced

2 red (bell) peppers, deeseeded and chopped into 2cm/¾ in cubes

1 aubergine (eggplant), chopped into 2cm/¾ in cubes

1 courgette (zucchini), chopped into 2cm/¾ in cubes

400g/14oz/scant 2 cups tinned chickpeas, drained and rinsed

55g/2oz/scant ¼ cup tomato purée (paste)

400g/14oz/scant 1⅔ cups tinned chopped tomatoes

3 tsp ground cumin

2 tsp paprika

½ tsp chilli powder

½ tsp freshly ground black pepper

1 large handful of parsley leaves, finely chopped

sea salt

To serve
1 lemon, cut into wedges
1 bag of mixed salad leaves

TARRAGON, GOAT'S CHEESE & WALNUT TART

SERVES 2
READY IN 25 MINUTES

1 green chilli, deseeded

3 spring onions (scallions),
    trimmed

55g/2oz/scant ⅓ cup pitted
    green olives

55g/2oz/scant ½ cup walnuts

1 large handful of tarragon
    leaves

125g/4½oz soft goat's cheese

¼ tsp paprika

1 lemon

2 tbsp olive oil

3 sheets of filo pastry, defrosted
    if frozen

100g/3½oz/heaped ⅓ cup
    yogurt

sea salt and freshly ground black
    pepper

MY GOAT'S CHEESE TART IS A TWIST ON THE CLASSIC
TURKISH SNACK BOREK. I HAVE MADE ONE LARGE TART
INSTEAD OF FIDDLY INDIVIDUAL PORTIONS, AND STUFFED
IT WITH CHILLI, SPRING ONIONS, OLIVES, WALNUTS,
TARRAGON, GOAT'S CHEESE AND PAPRIKA.

1 Preheat the oven to 180°C/350°F/Gas 4. Put the chilli
and spring onions (scallion) into a food processor, and
add the olives, walnuts and tarragon. Blend until coarsely
chopped, then add the goat's cheese and paprika. Squeeze
in the juice of ½ lemon and season with salt and pepper.
Give it a quick blast to mix it all together.

2 Take a piece of baking parchment, large enough to fit in
a baking tray, and scrunch it between your hands – this stops
the sides from curling up. Flatten the baking parchment on
to a chopping board and brush with olive oil. Lay a piece of
the filo pastry on top of the baking parchment and brush it
all over with oil (cover the unused filo with a damp tea towel
to prevent it from drying out). Put another piece of filo pastry
over the top and brush it with oil.

3 Scoop the filling into the centre of the pastry and spread
it out into a rectangular shape about 1.5cm/⅝in thick. Cover
with the final sheet of filo pastry and fold in the sides to form
a neat rectangle. Brush the top of the tart with oil and season
with salt and pepper.

4 Transfer the tart to the baking tray, by lifting up the sides
of the baking parchment, then bake for 15–18 minutes until
golden on top. Meanwhile, put the yogurt into a serving bowl,
squeeze in the juice from the remaining ½ lemon and season
with salt and pepper. Mix well. Serve the hot tart with the
lemony yogurt.

HERB & SPICE PILAF

1 Heat a large frying pan or skillet over a medium heat. Add the cashew nuts and gently toast, shaking the pan constantly, for 1–2 minutes. Add the flaked almonds and continue to shake the pan for a further 1–2 minutes, or until both the cashew nuts and almonds start turning golden. Transfer the nuts to a plate and set aside.

2 Put the cardamom pods on a chopping board and, using the flat side of a knife, press down until they split open and reveal their seeds. This will help to release their flavour. Heat the oil in a large frying pan over a medium heat, then add the split cardamom pods and the cumin seeds. Stir-fry for 10–20 seconds, or until the seeds start to crackle, then add the onion and fry, stirring occasionally, for 3–4 minutes, or until the onion is soft.

3 Put the rice into a large saucepan, cover with cold water and stir, and then set aside for 5 minutes to soak. Tip the rice into a colander and give it a really good rinse under the cold tap, until the water coming out of the rice runs clear. This washes the starch out of the rice and ensures you get lovely separated grains.

4 Tip the washed rice back into the saucepan and place over a medium heat. Add the onion and spice mixture and stir in the hot stock. Bring to the boil, cover, reduce the heat to low and simmer gently for 10–15 minutes, or until all the water has been absorbed and the rice is almost cooked but still has a little bite. Remove from the heat and remove the saucepan lid. Place a clean tea towel over the rice, then replace the lid and set aside to steam for 5–10 minutes.

5 Fluff up the rice with a fork and toss together with the toasted nuts, parsley and coriander (cilantro). Season with a really good pinch of salt and pepper, drizzle over a little oil, add a few coriander (cilantro) sprigs as a finishing touch and serve hot or warm.

SERVES 4
READY IN 45 MINUTES

55g/2oz/½ cup flaked almonds
55g/2oz/heaped ⅓ cup cashew nuts
2 cardamom pods
2 tbsp olive oil, plus extra for drizzling
2 tsp cumin seeds
1 large onion, finely chopped
350g/12oz/1¾ cups basmati rice
600ml/21fl oz/scant 2½ cups chicken or vegetable stock
2 large handfuls parsley leaves, finely chopped
2 large handfuls coriander (cilantro) leaves, finely chopped, plus extra sprigs to serve
sea salt and freshly ground black pepper

CRISPY ZAATAR HALLOUMI

SERVES 2
READY IN 15 MINUTES

200g/7oz halloumi, cut into
    5mm/¼ in slices
2 tbsp olive oil
60g/2¼oz/⅓ cup couscous
juice from ½ lemon
1 red chilli, deseeded and finely
    chopped
1 handful of parsley leaves, finely
    chopped
1 tbsp capers, drained and finely
    chopped
1 tbsp olive oil
sea salt and freshly ground
    black pepper

For the zaatar
1 tbsp sumac
1 tbsp dried oregano
3 tsp sesame seeds

1 To make the zaatar, mix the sumac, oregano, sesame seeds and a good pinch of salt in a bowl.

2 Put half the zaatar in a large mixing bowl and tip in the couscous. Mix with a fork. Pour over 90ml/3fl oz/generous ⅓ cup warm water, cover with cling film (plastic wrap) and leave to one side to absorb the water. This will take about 10 minutes.

3 Press each slice of halloumi into the zaatar spices to cover with a thin layer on one side. Heat the oil in large frying pan or skillet over a medium heat. Add the halloumi, spice-side down, and fry for 2–3 minutes on each side until golden. Remove the pan from the heat and leave to one side while you finish the salad.

4 When the couscous has absorbed all the water, fluff it up with a fork, then add the olive oil and squeeze in the juice from the lemon. Chuck in the chopped chilli, parsley and capers, and add a pinch of salt, if needed, and pepper. Serve the couscous with the delicious fried halloumi.

DESSERTS & DRINKS

CARDAMOM & PISTACHIO KULFI

1 Pour the evaporated milk into a saucepan and bring to the boil over a medium heat. Tip in the cornflour (corn starch) and sugar, reduce the heat to low and whisk continuously until smooth. Continue to heat, stirring occasionally, for 5 minutes, or until the mixture is slightly thickened.

2 Meanwhile, split the cardamom pods by pressing down on them with the back of a knife. Scrape out the seeds, crush them with the back of the knife and then finely chop them. Add the seeds to the evaporated milk mixture, along with the pistachio nuts and cream and mix well.

3 Transfer the mixture to a small plastic container with a lid. Cover and freeze for 6 hours or overnight. Remove from the freezer about 20 minutes before serving so the kulfi has a chance to soften. Alternatively, set the kulfi in four moulds lined with clingfilm (plastic wrap).

SERVES 4
READY IN 15 MINUTES,
** PLUS FREEZING**

400ml/14fl oz/1½ cups
  evaporated milk
1 tbsp cornflour (corn starch)
60g/2¼oz/heaped ¼ cup caster
  (superfine) sugar
3 cardamom pods
20g/¾oz/scant ¼ cup unsalted
  pistachio nuts, sliced, plus
  extra to serve
100ml/3½fl oz/⅓ cup double
  (heavy) cream

SALTED CARAMEL CHOCOLATE SAUCE WITH VANILLA ICE CREAM

SERVES 4
READY IN 10 MINUTES

500ml/17fl oz tub of awesome vanilla ice cream
125g/4½oz/⅔ cup light brown sugar
60g/2¼oz butter
50ml/1¾fl oz/scant ¼ cup double (heavy) cream
100g/3½oz dark chocolate (85% cocoa solids)
sea salt
40g/1½oz/⅓ cup hazelnuts, roughly chopped, to serve

THIS IS PROBABLY THE BEST SAUCE EVER! A BOLD STATEMENT, I KNOW, BUT WHAT COULD BE BETTER THAN A WICKEDLY SWEET SALTED CARAMEL SAUCE, LOADED UP WITH RICH DARK CHOCOLATE AND SERVED WARM AND OOZING OVER VANILLA ICE CREAM? FIND AN ESPECIALLY GOOD VANILLA ICE CREAM TO DO THE SAUCE JUSTICE.

1 Take the vanilla ice cream out of the freezer to soften. Meanwhile, tip the sugar for the sauce into a saucepan and add 1½ tablespoons water. Bring to the boil over a high heat and cook for 2–3 minutes, shaking the pan occasionally, until all the sugar has dissolved. Roughly chop the nuts while the sugar dissolves.

2 Remove the pan from the heat and add the butter. Return the pan to a low heat and melt the butter, whisking continuously. Continue to whisk for another 1 minute, or until the caramel turns light brown. Add a good pinch of salt and whisk well. Pour in the cream and continue to whisk until velvety smooth.

3 Break up the chocolate into the sauce and whisk continuously until completely melted and the sauce has thickened a little. Carefully pour the sauce into a heatproof jug and serve immediately with the ice cream and the hazelnuts to sprinkle over the top.

GOAN EXPLOSION TRUFFLES

ACTUAL TRUFFLES IN 30 MINUTES – GET IN! THE TRICK IS TO GET YOUR CAKE TIN REALLY COLD AND MAKE SURE THAT THE TRUFFLE MIX GOES INTO IT IN A THIN LAYER SO THAT IT SETS REALLY FAST. SCOOP OUT THE TRUFFLE MIX WITH A TEASPOON OR A FANCY MELON BALLER AND DROP EACH BALL INTO THE GROUND PISTACHIO NUTS FOR A SPEEDY COATING. COFFEE, CARDAMOM AND CHILLI FUNK UP THESE TRUFFLES. USE THE MADDEST, GREENEST PISTACHIOS YOU CAN FIND TO GET THE PERFECT GOAN EXPERIENCE.

SERVES 4
READY IN 30 MINUTES

1 handful of ice cubes
100ml/3½fl oz/generous ⅓ cup double (heavy) cream
15g/½oz butter
100g/3½oz dark chocolate (70% cocoa solids)
¼ tsp espresso powder
¼ tsp ground cardamom
a pinch of chilli powder
55g/2oz/heaped ⅓ cup shelled green pistachio nuts

1 Put the ice in a 25cm/10in cake tin with a fixed base and pop it into the freezer. Pour the cream into a small saucepan and add the butter. Cook over a medium heat for 2–3 minutes, stirring occasionally, until the butter melts.

2 Meanwhile, break up the chocolate into a microwaveproof bowl. Put it into the microwave and heat for 1 minute on high, or until the chocolate just starts to melt. (Alternatively, melt the chocolate in a heatproof bowl over a pan of gently simmering water, making sure the base of the bowl doesn't touch the water.) Remove the bowl from the microwave or steamer and add the espresso powder, cardamom and chilli powder. Pour over the hot cream and whisk together until thick and smooth.

3 Working as fast as you can, take the cake tin out of the freezer, discard the ice and wipe the tin dry with some kitchen paper. Pour the chocolate mixture into the tin and spread it out evenly in a thin layer, no deeper than 5mm/¼in, otherwise it won't set in time. Put the cake tin into the freezer and freeze for 20 minutes, or until set.

4 Chuck the nuts into a food processor and blend into a coarse rubble. Tip into a mixing bowl. Using a teaspoon or melon baller, scoop out the truffle mixture and drop each truffle ball into the bowl of crushed nuts and give the bowl a shake. Make sure all the truffles are coated, then tip into a bowl and serve.

DARK CHOCOLATE, CLOVE & CINNAMON BROWNIES

MAKES 16
READY IN 40 MINUTES, PLUS RESTING

250g/9oz unsalted butter, plus extra for greasing

300g/10½oz chocolate with 70–80% cocoa, plus extra to serve

125g/4½oz/heaped ½ cup caster (superfine) sugar

125g/4½oz/⅔ cup light muscovado sugar

3 eggs and 1 egg yolk, beaten

100g/3½oz/1 cup pecan nuts, crushed

60g/2¼oz/½ cup plain (all-purpose) flour

1 tsp baking powder

1 tsp sea salt

60g/2¼oz/scant ½ cup cocoa powder, plus extra to serve

¼ tsp ground cloves

½ tsp ground cinnamon, plus extra to serve

1 Preheat the oven to 180°C/350°F/Gas 4. Grease the bottom and sides of a 23cm/9in square cake tin, then line with baking parchment.

2 Break the chocolate into pieces and melt in a heatproof bowl set over a saucepan of barely simmering water. Make sure the bottom of the bowl doesn't touch the water. Once completely melted set aside to cool slightly.

3 Put the butter, caster (superfine) sugar and muscovado sugar into a food processor and blend on a high setting for about 5 minutes, or until they form a smooth paste.

4 Slowly add the eggs, a little at a time, to the butter and sugar mixture and blend on a low setting until everything is incorporated. Give the mixture a final blast on a high setting for 30 seconds, then transfer to a large mixing bowl.

5 Slowly fold in the melted chocolate, then add the nuts and sift in the flour, baking powder, salt, cocoa powder, cloves and cinnamon. Fold everything together using a large metal spoon, then scrape the batter into the prepared cake tin. Smooth the top with a palette knife and bake for 20–30 minutes, or until soft and gooey in the middle and just cracking on the top and sides. To test if the brownie is ready, insert a skewer into the centre pushing right to the bottom. It should come out with a little of the yummy, goey brownie clinging but not totally coating it. If the skewer is completely coated, put the brownie back in the oven and test it again every 3 minutes until cooked.

6 Remove from the oven and leave to cool for 30 minutes in the cake tin. Flip the brownie out of the tin onto a chopping board, peel off the baking parchment and cut into squares. Serve hot, warm or cold with a generous sprinkling of cocoa powder and a sprinkling of cinnamon, to taste.

PINEAPPLE & LIME PIE

RIGHT NOW, I AM IN LOVE WITH AMERICA, AND THIS PUDDING WAS INSPIRED BY THE AMERICAN CLASSIC, KEY LIME PIE. I HAVE USED PINEAPPLE, WITH A HINT OF CHILLI, INSTEAD OF THE TRADITIONAL LIME, PLUS A NO-BAKE BISCUIT BASE TO MAKE IT QUICK.

SERVES 4
READY IN 20 MINUTES

110g/3¾oz butter
½ pineapple
30g/1oz demerara (turbinado) sugar
a pinch of crushed chilli flakes
140g/5oz digestive biscuits
400ml/14fl oz/generous 1½ cups double (heavy) cream
2 tbsp icing (confectioners') sugar
½ lime

1 Put 80g/2¾oz of the butter in a small saucepan over a medium heat and the remaining butter in a small frying pan or skillet over a medium heat.

2 While the butter melts, cut the top and bottom off the pineapple, then stand it upright on your chopping board. Slice off the skin, cutting downwards from top to bottom. Carefully cut out any pieces of skin left on the fruit. Cut the pineapple half in half lengthways, then slice off the woody core so that you are left with the soft fruit. Cut the pineapple flesh into small pieces and add them to the small frying pan. Add the demerara (turbinado) sugar and a pinch of chilli flakes. Mix well and cook for 8–10 minutes, shaking the pan occasionally, until the pineapple starts to soften and the sauce has thickened. Remove from the heat and leave to one side to cool a little.

3 Put the biscuits into a food processor and blend into a fine powder while the pineapple cooks. Tip into a mixing bowl and pour over the melted butter from the small saucepan. Mix well. Line the base and sides of a 19cm/7½in springform cake tin with baking parchment and press the biscuit mix into the base, using the back of a spoon. Put the cake tin into the fridge to chill while you whisk the cream.

4 Pour the cream into a large mixing bowl and add the icing (confectioners') sugar. Zest in the lime, squeeze in the juice, then whisk into firm peaks. Remove the cake tin from the fridge and fill with the cream. Top with the pineapple pieces, drizzle over the sauce from the pineapple, then open the side of the cake tin, remove the paper and serve.

MANGO & VANILLA COCONUT POTS

SERVES 4
READY IN 10 MINUTES

2 ripe mangoes
4 tbsp icing (confectioners')
   sugar
juice of ½ orange
300ml/10½fl oz/scant 1¼ cups
   double (heavy) cream
70ml/2¼fl oz/generous ¼ cup
   coconut cream
1 tsp vanilla extract

COCONUT AND MANGO ARE BEST MATES AND APPEAR IN VARIOUS GUISES IN SOUTH-EAST ASIAN DESSERTS. THESE FRESH LITTLE PUDDINGS ARE INSPIRED BY THE MANY VARIETIES I HAVE EATEN OVER THE YEARS. I HAVE MADE MY VERSION TO BE AS QUICK AS POSSIBLE WITHOUT CUTTING BACK ON ANY FLAVOUR. THE MANGO IS SQUISHED TOGETHER WITH SUGAR AND ORANGE TO SOFTEN IT AND INTENSIFY THE TASTE. THE SWEET FRUIT IS THEN TOPPED OFF WITH LUSCIOUS CREAM THAT HAS BEEN WHIPPED WITH COCONUT CREAM TO ADD THAT AUTHENTIC ASIAN TWIST.

1 Cut off the mango peel, then slice off the flesh from the sides and around the stone. Chop into bite-sized pieces, then put them in a mixing bowl.

2 Add half the icing (confectioners') sugar and the orange juice. Mix together using your hands to slightly break up the mango, then leave to one side.

3 Pour the double (heavy) cream into a mixing bowl and whisk into firm peaks. Add the coconut cream, remaining icing sugar and the vanilla extract, and whisk together. To serve, divide the mango mixture into four glasses and top each one with the cream.

PUMPKIN, CHOCOLATE & WALNUTS

THIS IS MY VERSION OF A CLASSIC TURKISH DESSERT OF SLOW-BRAISED PUMPKIN SERVED WITH WALNUTS. MY TWIST IS TO ADD CHUNKS OF BITTER DARK CHOCOLATE, WHICH MELT INTO THE SWEET PUMPKIN, TOPPED WITH LOVELY SOFT WHIPPED CREAM.

SERVES 4
READY IN 25 MINUTES

750g/1lb 10oz pumpkin
125ml/4fl oz/½ cup double (heavy) cream
25g/1oz butter
55g/2oz/¼ cup demerara (turbinado) sugar
6 cloves
25g/1oz dark chocolate (70% cocoa solids)
55g/2oz/scant ½ cup walnuts

1 Peel and deseed the pumpkin and cut it into 2.5cm/1in pieces. Chuck them into a microwaveproof bowl and add 100ml/3½fl oz/generous ⅓ cup water. Cover with cling film (plastic wrap) and microwave on high for 10 minutes, or until the pieces are soft but haven't turned to mush. To check, poke them with a sharp knife – it should slide out very easily.

2 Whip the cream to soft peaks while the pumpkin cooks, and leave to one side. Put the butter, sugar and cloves in a frying pan or skillet, and heat over a low heat. Once the sugar starts to look a bit dry, shake the pan and it will suddenly dissolve into a liquid. Once completely dissolved, remove from the heat – it will look as though it has split from the butter, but don't worry, I promise it's meant to look like this.

3 Cut two-thirds of the chocolate into tiny pieces and divide into 4 portions. Scrunch the walnuts between your hands over a bowl so that they break up into small pieces.

4 Using a slotted spoon, carefully transfer the cooked pumpkin to the frying pan with the sugar mixture. Cook over a low heat for 5 minutes, stirring occasionally.

5 Add all but 1 tablespoon of the crushed walnuts to the pumpkin and mix everything together. Spoon the pumpkin into four heatproof glasses, picking out the cloves as you go. Scatter a pile of chocolate over each one and spoon over a quarter of the cream. Sprinkle over the remaining walnuts and grate the last of the chocolate over the top. Serve immediately, so that the chocolate oozes through the pudding.

CINNAMON FIG TARTS

SERVES 4
READY IN 25 MINUTES

flour, for dusting
150g/5½oz puff pastry,
    defrosted if frozen
1 tsp demerara (turbinado) sugar
½ tsp ground cinnamon
¼ tsp ground ginger
6 small or 3 medium figs
250ml/9fl oz/1 cup double
    (heavy) cream
2 clementines
2 tbsp icing (confectioners')
    sugar
1 small handful of mint leaves

FIGS ARE A STAPLE ELEMENT OF DESSERTS ACROSS
THE MIDDLE EAST, ADDING COLOUR, FLAVOUR AND TEXTURE,
AND THEY WORK BEAUTIFULLY WITH SPICES. I HAVE OFTEN
SEEN THE HUMBLE FIG TRANSFORMED INTO A SPECTACULAR
DISH, AND IT'S PERFECT FOR A QUICK DESSERT. BAKING FIGS
INTENSIFIES THEIR FLAVOUR, SO I'VE LAID THEM ON PUFF
PASTRY THAT WAS SPRINKLED WITH DEMERARA (TURBINADO)
SUGAR, CINNAMON AND GROUND GINGER. WHEN COOKED,
THEY ARE WRAPPED IN A WONDERFUL, SWEET BLANKET.
THE CLEMENTINE AND MINT CREAM FRESHENS UP THE
FLAVOURS AND ACCENTUATES THE WARMTH OF THE SPICES.

1 Preheat the oven to 200°C/400°F/Gas 6. Line a baking
    sheet with baking parchment. Scrunch it up in your hands
    and smooth it out to stop it rolling up.

2 Flour the work surface and roll out the pastry to just under
    5mm/¼in thick. Cut the pastry into 4 rectangles, measuring
    10 × 15cm/4 × 6in, and put them on to the baking parchment.
    Prick each one a few times with a fork.

3 Mix the demerara (turbinado) sugar, cinnamon and ginger
    in a bowl, then sprinkle evenly over each pastry. Cut the small
    figs in half, or the medium figs into quarters, and put 3 pieces
    of fig down the centre of each rectangle. Bake the tarts for
    18–20 minutes until puffed and golden.

4 Meanwhile, pour the cream into a large mixing bowl. Zest in
    of 1 of the clementines and squeeze in the juice of both. Sift
    in the icing (confectioners') sugar, then whip the cream until
    it forms soft peaks. Save a few mint leaves for decoration
    and finely chop the remainder. Fold the chopped mint leaves
    into the cream. Serve the hot tarts with a large dollop of the
    cream and a scattering of mint leaves.

STRAWBERRY LAYER CAKES

THESE AWESOME CRISPY, CREAMY STRAWBERRY LAYER
CAKES ARE A NOD TO MY TIME IN MOROCCO. CINNAMON,
ORANGE AND VANILLA ADD THE EXOTIC FLAVOURS AND
TURN THIS DESSERT INTO SOMETHING OUT OF THE ORDINARY.

SERVES 4
READY IN 25 MINUTES

350g/12oz/2⅓ cups
    strawberries
½ tsp ground cinnamon, plus
    little extra for dusting
3 tbsp icing (confectioners')
    sugar
½ orange
2 large sheets of filo pastry,
    defrosted if frozen
300g/10½oz/scant 1¼ cups
    full-fat Greek yogurt
1 tsp vanilla extract
55g/2oz/scant ½ cup walnut
    pieces

1 Slice the strawberries, discarding their tops, and put them in
a shallow dish. Sprinkle over the cinnamon and 1 tablespoon
of the icing sugar. Squeeze over the juice from the orange
and mix well. Cover and leave to one side.

2 Cut the filo pastry into 12 rectangles, each measuring
8 × 12cm/3¼ × 4½in (and cover the filo with a damp tea
towel to prevent it from drying out). Heat a large frying pan
or skillet over a medium-high heat and pan-fry the filo pastry
in batches until golden and crispy. This will take about 1–1½
minutes on one side and 30 seconds–1 minute on the other.
Remove from the pan and put carefully to one side.

3 Put the yogurt in a mixing bowl while cooking the filo,
and add the remaining icing sugar and the vanilla. Whisk
everything together well and leave to one side.

4 When all the filo is cooked you can construct the cakes.
Put a piece of cooked filo on to a serving plate and add
a spoonful of yogurt on top. Spread it out and cover with
a thin layer of strawberries. Put another piece of filo over
the strawberries, and then repeat with more yogurt and
another layer of strawberries. Put a third piece of filo over
the strawberries, spread a spoonful of yogurt over the top,
then break up some of the walnuts and scatter them over.
Add a pinch of cinnamon, then repeat for the other 3 layer
cakes. Serve with any remaining strawberries.

SHENYANG HONEY & SESAME BANANAS

SERVES 4
READY IN 15 MINUTES

sunflower oil, for shallow-frying
150g/5½oz/scant 1¼ cups plain
   (all-purpose) flour
2 tbsp icing (confectioners')
   sugar
¾ tsp ground cloves
¾ tsp chilli powder
55g/2oz/heaped ⅓ cup sesame
   seeds
1 egg
2 bananas
3 tbsp clear honey

I HAVE CREATED A REALLY QUICK VERSION OF THE TASTY SNACK FROM THAT UNDERGROUND HIGH STREET IN SHENYANG. SESAME SEEDS AND FLOUR FORM THE BASE OF A BATTER TO COAT THE BANANAS, AND IT'S FLAVOURED WITH WARMING GROUND CLOVES AND CHILLI POWDER. THE FLAVOUR OF THE SPICES LINGERS WHEN THE BANANAS ARE COOKED, AND IT'S SOMEHOW EXAGGERATED BY THE RUNNY HONEY DRIZZLED OVER BEFORE SERVING. THIS IS EXPRESS COOKING AT ITS BEST.

1 Pour the oil into a saucepan to a depth of 1.5cm/⅝in and heat over a medium-high heat. Meanwhile, sift the flour, icing sugar, cloves and chilli powder into a large mixing bowl, and add 30g/1oz/scant ¼ cup of the sesame seeds. Crack in the egg, then slowly whisk in 200ml/7fl oz/scant 1 cup cold water to form a smooth batter.

2 Peel the bananas and cut them into 1cm/½in pieces. Put the pieces into the batter and carefully transfer them to the hot oil using a pair of tongs. Fry the bananas for 30–45 seconds on each side until beautifully golden and crispy.

3 Remove the bananas from the pan and put them on kitchen paper to drain. Transfer the bananas to a serving plate and drizzle over the honey. Scatter over the remaining sesame seeds and serve.

MANGO, ORANGE & NUTMEG CHEESECAKE

CHEESECAKE IS LUSCIOUS TO EAT BUT CAN BE TRICKY TO MAKE. THIS IS A VERY SIMPLE VERSION THAT INVOLVES A BIT OF MIXING AND THEN LOTS OF EATING. THE MAIN FLAVOURS ARE FRESH MANGO AND ORANGE, WHICH ARE COMPLEMENTED BY FRESHLY GRATED NUTMEG, WHICH BRINGS OUT THE SWEETNESS OF THE MANGO. .

SERVES 8–10
READY IN 45 MINUTES, PLUS RESTING

100g/3½oz unsalted butter, plus extra for greasing
200g/7oz digestive biscuits
1 tbsp caster (superfine) sugar
1 large mangoes, peeled, pitted and cut into chunks
50ml/1½oz/3 tbsp orange juice
900g/2lb cream cheese
100g/3½oz/heaped ¾ cup icing (confectioners') sugar
¼ fresh nutmeg, finely grated, plus extra for sprinkling

1 Grease the sides and base of a 20 x 10cm/8 x 4in non-stick springform cake tin and line the base with baking parchment. Put the digestive biscuits into a food processor and blend to a fine crumb. Tip the biscuit crumbs into a saucepan and rinse the food processor bowl.

2 Add the butter and caster (superfine) sugar to the crumb mix, place over a medium heat and mix together until the butter and sugar has melted completely. Tip the biscuit mixture into the prepared cake tin, then push it down, using a spoon, to form an even layer across the base. Refrigerate for 30 minutes.

3 Meanwhile, put the mango and orange juice into a food processor bowl and blend to a purée. Pass the purée through a sieve and divide the mixture in two. Cover one portion and refrigerate to serve with the cheesecake when it's ready and return the other portion to the food processor bowl.

4 Put the cream cheese, icing (confectioners') sugar, freshly grated nutmeg into the food processor bowl with the mango and orange purée and blend until smooth.

5 Scrape the cheese and mango mixture over the biscuit base in the cake tin and refrigerate for 8 hours or overnight. When you are ready to serve, pop open the springform mechanism on the cake tin, carefully remove the sides and slowly slip the cake off the bottom onto a serving plate. Sprinkle with finely grated fresh nutmeg, drizzle over the remaining mango and orange purée and serve.

MEXICAN CINNAMON PEACHES

SERVES 4
READY IN 1 HOUR

180g/6¼oz/heaped ¾ cup
   caster (superfine) sugar
7.5cm/3in cinnamon stick
4 ripe peaches
juice of 1 lemon
vanilla ice cream, to serve
   (optional)

1 Put the sugar and cinnamon into a large saucepan with 500ml/17fl oz/2 cups water, then bring to the boil over a medium heat until all the sugar has dissolved. Reduce the heat to low and simmer for 10 minutes.

2 Carefully add the peaches, cover and cook, turning occasionally, for 5 minutes until they start to soften. Remove the peaches and set aside for about 10 minutes. Once cool enough to handle, peel off the skins and put the skins back into the syrup, along with the lemon juice. The peach skins will give the syrup a lovely pink colour. Simmer for 5 minutes, then remove the cinnamon and simmer for a further 13–15 minutes, or until the syrup has reduced right down and is really sticky.

3 Cut the peaches in half and gently tear the flesh away from the stones with your hands so it breaks into rough pieces. This will give you a great rustic look, rather than doing it neatly with a knife. Pour over the fragrant syrup and serve immediately with vanilla ice cream, if liked.

CHILLI & LIME FRUIT SALAD

1 Put the sugar, cinnamon, star anise and chilli flakes into a large pan with 250ml/9fl oz/1 cup water and bring to the boil over a high heat. Stir continuously for 1 minute, or until all the sugar has dissolved, then reduce the heat to medium and simmer, shaking the pan occasionally, for 10 minutes until the liquid has reduced to a thin syrup. Transfer the syrup to a mixing bowl and set aside to cool. Remove the cinnamon to stop its flavour overpowering the dressing, but reserve for decoration.

2 Once the syrup has cooled, pour in the lime juice and passion fruit and mix well. Add the mango, pineapple and papaya, then toss together so that the spicy, sweet-sour flavours of the dressing coat the fruit.

3 Serve at room temperature or chilled with a generous dollop of yogurt and the star anise and cinnamon arranged on top.

SERVES 4
READY IN 50 MINUTES

90g/3¼oz/heaped ⅓ cup caster (superfine) sugar
5cm/2in cinnamon stick
2 star anise
¼ tsp chilli flakes
juice of 2 limes
seeds and pulp of 3 passion fruit
1 mango, peeled, pitted and roughly chopped
½ pineapple, peeled, cored and roughly chopped
1 papaya, peeled, deseeded and roughly chopped
natural yogurt, to serve

VANILLA & HONEY SYLLABUB

SERVES 4
READY IN 40 MINUTES

300ml/10½fl oz/generous 1 cup
double (heavy) cream
3 tbsp honey, plus extra to
serve (optional)
juice of 2 lemons
zest of 1 lemon
100ml/3½fl oz/⅓ cup natural
yogurt
1 vanilla pod
80g/2¾oz/½ cup unsalted
pistachio nuts, shelled and
roughly chopped

SYLLABUBS ARE ACTUALLY VERY OLD BRITISH DESSERTS THAT
DATE ALL THE WAY BACK TO THE TUDORS. TRADITIONALLY,
THEY WERE A MIX OF CREAM AND WINE, THOUGHT TO BE
SHOWSTOPPERS WHEN SERVED AT FANCY PARTIES. I HAVE
MODERNIZED MY VERSION WITH VANILLA, AND HAVE USED A
LITTLE YOGURT TO KEEP IT REALLY LIGHT. THE SWEET HONEY
AND REFRESHING LEMON GET THE MOUTH WATERING, WHILE
THE VIVID GREEN PISTACHIOS PROVIDE JUST THE RIGHT
AMOUNT OF COLOUR AND CRUNCH – DEFINITELY STILL A
DESSERT TO BE NOTICED!

1 Pour the cream into a large mixing bowl and whisk into firm
peaks using a handheld electric whisk.

2 In a separate small bowl, whisk the honey and lemon juice
together until well combined, then add the lemon zest and
yogurt and mix well.

3 Using a sharp knife, split the vanilla pod in half, scrape the
seeds into the yogurt mixture and mix until well combined.

4 Fold the yogurt into the cream using a metal spoon, then
divide the mixture into four glasses or bowls and refrigerate
for at least 30 minutes. Serve drizzled with honey, if liked, and
pistachios sprinkled over the top.

HOT & SPICY BOURBON

BOURBON HAS BEEN MY DRINK OF THE MONTH FOR QUITE SOME TIME NOW. IT HAS A GOOD SMOKY FLAVOUR THAT COMES FROM THE CHARRED OAK BARRELS IT IS AGED IN. THE HOT, STICKY KENTUCKY AIR SPEEDS UP THIS AGEING PROCESS, SO THE BOURBON ENDS UP BEING A RELATIVELY YOUNG DRINK. THIS GIVES IT A BEAUTIFULLY SMOOTH AND MELLOW TASTE. AS YOU CAN TELL, I AM QUITE INTO IT! IN THIS DELICIOUS HOT DRINK THE STAR ANISE, CINNAMON AND CLOVES ACCENTUATE THE TASTE OF THE BOURBON, AND THE ORANGE AND HONEY PROVIDE THE CLASSIC ACCOMPANYING FLAVOURS. THIS IS ADVANCED HOT-TODDY DRINKING, PEOPLE!

SERVES 4
READY IN 5 MINUTES

4 star anise
4 cinnamon sticks
8 cloves
1 orange
250ml/9fl oz/1 cup bourbon
4 tbsp clear honey

1 Boil the kettle. Meanwhile, divide the star anise, cinnamon sticks and cloves into four mugs.

2 Using a peeler, peel 4 strips of orange zest, give them a twist and add them to the mugs. Slice 4 slices from the orange and put one in each mug.

3 Divide the Bourbon and honey into the mugs, then fill each one to the top with boiling water. Stir each mug of hot and spicy bourbon with a cinnamon stick and serve.

LEMONGRASS, GINGER & RUM COCKTAILS

SERVES 4
READY IN 40 MINUTES

4 lemongrass stalks
250g/9oz/heaped 1 cup caster
    (superfine) sugar
1cm/½in piece root ginger,
    peeled and grated
100ml/3½fl oz/ ⅓ cup light rum
juice of 2 limes
tonic water, for topping up

1 Cut off the ends of the lemongrass stalks and bash the fatter ends of the lemongrass a couple of times with a heavy spoon to help release their delicious flavour. Put the lemongrass in a saucepan with the sugar and 185ml/6fl oz/¾ cup water and bring to the boil. Turn the heat down to low and simmer, shaking the pan occasionally, for 4–5 minutes, or until all the sugar has dissolved. Remove from the heat and set aside to cool. You will end up with more sugar syrup than you need for four drinks, but it's important to cover the lemongrass stalks with enough water so you get the maximum flavour from them. The extra syrup will keep for a few days in the refrigerator.

2 Put the ginger into a cocktail shaker, discarding any fibrous bits. Pour in the rum, juice from 1 of the limes, 55ml/1¾fl oz/scant ¼ cup of the cooled lemongrass sugar syrup, then add the lemongrass stalks from the syrup and a handful of ice. Shake vigorously until the ingredients are well combined.

3 Divide the cocktail into four ice-filled rocks glasses, top up each glass with tonic water and serve with a lemongrass stalk from the shaker to use as a stirrer.

4 Squeeze the juice from the remaining lime into the four glasses and stir in with the lemongrass stalks. Serve immediately.

INDEX